LUCKY BY CHOICE

The 52 Laws of Making Successful, Life-Changing Decisions

"You Decide Your Destiny"

by
Keio Gamble

LUCKY BY CHOICE:
The 52 Laws of Making Successful, Life-Changing Decisions

Copyright © 2017 by **Keio Gamble**

All rights reserved. No part of this book may be reproduced or transmitted in any form or by any means -- electronic, mechanical, photocopy, recording, scanning, or by any information storage and retrieval system – except for brief quotations in critical reviews or articles, without written permission of the author.

All rights reserved for translation into foreign languages.

ISBN 978-0-9990136-0-1   Paperback
ISBN 978-0-9990136-1-8   Hardback
ISBN 978-0-9990136-2-5   Audio Book
ISBN 978-0-9990136-3-2   eBook

Library of Congress Control Number: 2017907339

Printed in the United States of America

For information regarding bulk purchases and/or special discounts for educational purposes:

Lucky By Choice, LLC
PO Box 411395
Dallas, Texas 75241

www.luckybychoice.com

Dedication

This book is dedicated to YOU, the reader.

The fact that you have this book in your hands speaks volumes about you and your journey in life.

I want to sincerely thank you for this time you are giving me while reading my body of work.

Today is the first day of the rest of your life.
Make the rest of your life the best of your life.

Acknowledgments

First and foremost, I want to say to all mentioned below; "I never would have made it, without you."

To my family: Donna Depron [Mother], Edward Hudspeth [Father], Kevan Wise [Son], Zack Jones [Son], Trinette Fannin [Sister], Tanetta Rogers [Sister], Edwin Archie [Brother], Ruby Hudspeth [Grandmother], T.L. Hudspeth [Grandfather], Shairis Patterson [Niece], Darvontre Gamble [Nephew], Gerry Gamble [Uncle], Cheryl Rosebud [Aunt], Kentrail Elder [Cousin], Antonio Miller [Cousin], Maronica Rosebud [Cousin], Bruce Gamble [Cousin], Jacqueline Gamble [Cousin], Tammy Miller [Cousin] and a host of other relatives; I thank you from the bottom of my heart for the sacrifices you have made for me over the years. I thank you for the times when I couldn't, and you could. I thank you for allowing me to be who I have become today.

In addition to my family, the following people have supported my dreams, gave me a shoulder to cry on when I felt defeated, loaned me money when I was in need, invested in my bright ideas, encouraged me when my spirits were low, provided life experiences that birthed the content that you are about to read, or partnered with me in some influential way while on my journey to success.

So without further delay, in no particular order, I thank Attorney Ricky Anderson, Charles Key, Craig Sweet, Shirley Thomas, Kira Lane, Josh Cisneros, Elise Portley, Willie Hinchen, Senator Royce West, Kristi Adam, Dwaina Brooks, Stefanie Brooks, April Wise, Asiah Jacobs, Chris Lytle, Mike "Mic Moodswing" Senters, Mike "360" Brooks, Carlos "Chulo" Correa, LiQuande James, Corey Phifer, Nikki Smith, James Gibson, Sugar Ray Destin, Jr., Tiffany Woody, Marcus Payne,

Clarence Williams, Attorney David Small, Kyland Dobbins, David Woodard, Demetrius Early, Dave Bundrick, Larrah Carroll, Khayyan "Don Chief" Curtis, Bridgette Grosvenor, Yanika Daniels, Derryl Williams, Carlton Dixon, Marcus Wright, Isaiah "Young Geno" Thomas, Telly Green, Eric "Victory" Johnson, D'Anthony Mims, Bryan Couch, Bubba Washington, Jr., Ericka Woods, Matt Rojas, Tenea Lowery, and Frazier "Trae tha Truth" Thompson, III.

To my Brothers of Omega Psi Phi Fraternity, Incorporated; especially my birth chapter [Rho Theta] and my line Brothers [Unseen 13, Spring 1996]....thank you for your time, patience, and unselfish friendship. With you, I've learned that friendship is essential to the soul. I've learned to be my Brother's keeper. I've learned that there is such a thing as humility with dignity. I've learned what the crux of the whole matter is. I value what it costs to be a friend, and what it takes as well. Being thoroughly immersed in the true Omega spirit of Manhood, Scholarship, Perseverance, and Uplift; through days of joy or years of pain, to serve thee e'er will be my aim.

For those that are unable to read this, but I still owe them recognition......Melva Chiles [Maternal Grandmother], Charles Finley [Maternal Grandfather], Kenneth Gamble [Uncle], Kenneth Miller [Cousin], Jason Rosebud [Cousin], Dushon Arrington, Michael Love, Casey Parker, Weslyn "Mama Wes" Monroe, and Jarami Thomas. You may be gone, but definitely not forgotten. May you all continue to rest in peace, and your spirits live forever.

You all have been an inspiration to me and a driving force for me at some of the most pivotal places in my life. For your beliefs in me, contributions to me, and support of me; from deep down in my soul, I sincerely thank you.

If you are reading this and I forgot to acknowledge you, please charge it to my brain and not my heart.

Special Thanks To……..

Gerry Robert, Bonnie Canesso, JG Francoeur, Evan Robert, Andreea Mihalcea, Shirley Salumbides, Daisy Gamboa, Sean Irrol, and the rest of the Black Card Books staff for my awesome book cover, your expert guidance, and magnificent mentoring.

Table of Contents

Preface 1
Introduction 3

Part One: KNOW THYSELF

1. The Man In The Mirror 9
2. As A Man Thinketh 11
3. The Showroom Car 17
4. Try & Let Go 23
5. Is That For Me? 29
6. Check Your Expectations 35
7. Perception Is Reality 39
8. I Can't Sleep 45
9. Purpose & Reason 51
10. Beyond The Basics 57
11. Birds Of A Feather 63
12. Who Do You Believe In? 69
13. What's Your Story? 71

Part Two: EXECUTIVE DECISIONS

14. Thinking For A Change 77
15. G-14 Classified 79
16. Tomorrow Never Comes... 83
17. Change Your Words, Change Your World 89
18. What Happened?... 93
19. The F Word 99
20. More Than Money 105
21. It's Not About You 111
22. Above Reproach 115
23. Consequences & Repercussions............................ 119
24. Black & White.. 123
25. Does Size Matter? 127
26. Conversation Ruled The Nation,
But Understanding Conquered The World 129

Part Three: THE WINNERS' CIRCLE

27. Wax On, Wax Off 135
28. Play To Win 139
29. Tune In To Your Star Player 143
30. Difficult Takes A Day, Impossible Takes A Week 151
31. The Harder I Work, The Luckier I Get 157
32. Keep Yourself In Fighting Trim 161
33. You Miss 100% Of The Shots You Don't Take 167
34. The Fortune Is In The Follow Through 173
35. Lose Yourself 177
36. Take Charge! 183
37. Ordinary vs EXTRA-Ordinary 187
38. Do It Again 193
39. Who Gave You The Right To Quit? 195

Part Four: SUCCESS IS A JOURNEY, NOT A DESTINATION

40. Chance Favors The Prepared Mind 201
41. Are We There Yet? 203
42. There Is No Plan B 207
43. Location, Location, Location 213
44. The Law Of The Harvest 219
45. The Bridge Builder 225
46. Write Out Loud! 229
47. Staying Ready To Keep From Getting Ready ... 235
48. Neither Should Be Wasted 239
49. You Get What You Negotiate 245
50. Knew Better, Do Better 249
51. Nobody Owes You Anything 253
52. The Choice Is Yours 257

About The Author 261

Preface

We've all heard the saying, "if it wasn't for bad luck, I wouldn't have any." At one point, I really believed that.

I started this journey a little over 10 years ago. One day, I was analyzing my life and came to the conclusion that if it wasn't for bad luck, I wouldn't have any. Then it hit me. I was dead wrong!! My supposed "luck" was a direct result of the decisions I had made up to that point. It was then that I had my inner revelation. With no hesitation, I immediately began another course on my life's journey. In that very moment, things became clearer. I started to notice that my thought process was very flawed and I wanted change. I needed change.

Dreams of me flying occupied my nights many times. What did that mean? I'm still not sure to this day, but this I do know. It was such a liberating experience. Funny enough, as far back as I can remember; I really enjoyed my flights. I can remember soaring high over the city, feeling the wind beneath me. I had no cape, no wings. All it ever took for me to take off was a running start, and up, up, up and away I went. I had one problem. My landing was rough. As the years went by, I figured out that my approach was all wrong. The reason I never landed smoothly was because my approach was flawed, and uncalculated. I was a great starter, but terrible finisher. I was an awesome visionary, but mediocre executioner. To me, I was able to translate that into my reality. My perception. My interpretation. My mindset. The way I thought. The decisions I made.

By definition, approach is the way of dealing with something. Deep down, I was unhappy with the way I was dealing with life. On the outside, all seemed well; but on the inside, I was falling apart. Just as a pilot has to do when landing a plane, we must be able to approach our landings in life by making the right decisions. We must have a plan of action, a mapped-out course, and an attitude that reflects the altitudes we desire to reach in life.

To keep my mindset in alignment with my goals, I adopted a five-star platform to sturdy my foundation. Dedication, Discipline, Excellence, Integrity, and Respect became the principles in which I live by. Through these principles, I manage my approach on life, my choices, and my decisions.

Every beginning has an end. You have the ultimate right to decide what yours is.

LUCK didn't choose me, I CHOSE IT!!! I choose to be lucky by the choices that I make, and the actions that I take.

Introduction

The revelation of self worth is too prevalent and powerful of a phenomenon to overlook. You are the master of your fate, and the captain of your soul.

The foundation of this book sits on the theory of progressive transformation through self revelation, mental expansion, and personal development.

This book is broken down into 4 parts and 52 chapters. The 4 parts symbolize the 4 seasons, and the 52 chapters reflect the 52 weeks in a year. The parts and chapters are a direct reflection on how the seasons and weeks govern our daily lives.

I will introduce you to "The 52 Laws of Making Successful, Life-Changing Decisions" through the steps of self assessment [Part One: Know Thyself], moral compassing [Part Two: Executive Decisions], mindset shifting [Part Three: The Winners' Circle], and learning how to prepare to receive [Part Four: Success Is A Journey, Not A Destination].

I challenge you to live with this book for a year. One week at a time, one chapter per week. Of course some of you will be like me, and won't be able to put a good book down after the first chapter; and will go ahead and finish it in a few days. After you do, keep it as a companion. Use this book as a reference on your journey of self revelation, mental expansion, and personal development.

As a bonus, I give to you 40 nuggets of wisdom as hidden gems in the book to digest during your gestation period in the form of quotes and poems. In many religious texts, 40 is a sacred number that represents transition or change, the time it takes for a new generation to arise, the concept of renewal, or a new beginning. I call it the cycle of creation.

In Christianity, before his temptation, Jesus fasted forty days and forty nights in the Judean desert [the observation and practice of Lent]. Forty days was the period from the resurrection of Jesus to the ascension of Jesus. Moses spent 40 days on Mount Sinai before receiving the 10 Commandments. Noah and the Ark withstood forty days and nights of rain. In Islam, Muhammad was 40 years old when he first received the revelation delivered by the archangel Gabriel. Muhammad prayed and fasted for 40 days in the cave. It is also said that a person's intellect attains maturity in forty years, everyone according to his own capacity. There is an Arabic proverb that says "to understand a people, you must live among them for 40 days." In Judaism, the Hebrew people lived in the Sinai desert for forty years. One of the prerequisites for a man to study Kabbalah is that he is forty years old. Even in Hinduism, the fasting periods are for 40 days. Aristotle believed that through ensoulment, it took 40 days for the human being to gain its soul. Likewise, in life itself, it takes 40 days for an embryo to be formed in its mother's womb; and it takes 40 weeks to be considered a full term pregnancy. Forty represents the most auspicious time for personal growth, development, and renewal.

So it should come as no surprise that I see it befitting to give you my 40. The contents of this book that I now share with you have brought me through my "40", my wilderness, my gestation, my journey, and my continuous quest for success.

As fate would have it, my time has come; I also turned 40 this year. The release date of this book is 40 weeks after my 40th birthday.

Second to the Bible, Qur'an/Koran, Vedas, Torah, or Talmud; this book will prove to be an essential guide to life-changing personal success.

Introduction

This is my dissertation.

Part One:

KNOW THYSELF

1. The Man In The Mirror

"To Thine Ownself Be True" is Polonius's last piece of advice to his son Laertes in the story of Hamlet, written by Shakespeare. So to you, it will be my first piece of advice. Now let's jump right in.

> *"I'm gonna make a change, for once in my life.*
> *It's gonna feel real good, gonna make a difference.*
> *Gonna make it right......."*

> *"I'm starting with the man in the mirror.*
> *I'm asking him to change his ways.*
> *And no message could have been any clearer.*
> *If you wanna make the world a better place,*
> *Take a look at yourself, and then make a change."*

The beginning lyrics to one of the greatest songs ever performed in my lifetime, "The Man In The Mirror", by Michael Jackson were the clearest instructions ever given in a song about the revelation of self worth and how prevalent and powerful of a phenomenon it is to overlook. It was one of the most critically acclaimed songs by MJ, and offered a straightforward homily of personal commitment. With its unparalleled, worldwide influence; it was a definite inspiration for me and the writing of this chapter, and why it is the first chapter of this book.

As I began my process of self assessment, I had to embrace the hard truth about where and who I was in life. I had to be real with myself. I couldn't lie to myself any longer. I was broke and broken, at the same time. I was in a deep, deep, deep hole. I decided to use some advice that I had been given......the best way to get out of a hole is to first stop digging; and so I did. Once I stopped digging and started to take self-inventory, I realized that I had learned to insulate myself from a lot of good, hard truths about who I was. Looking at myself in the mirror was very painful, but rewarding. I had to face the realization that I was my own worst enemy. I was in my own way. What do you do when the problem is you? Most people ignore it.

On that day, I declared war on myself. Taking absolute authority over my life became paramount. I became my own competition.

The day you decide to love yourself is the day you'll conquer the world. Life isn't about finding yourself. Life is about creating yourself. You must learn to take proper self-inventory, and begin self-investment. Going through the process of honest, self-assessment is the only way to the other side of success.

Your plan starts with you. Learn to prefer and accept all of the ugly truths over the pretty lies about yourself. Make the mirror your best friend, and you'll find some peace within. If you look inside, you'll find where your strength resides. Don't just compete with the old version of yourself, dominate it!

Muhammad Ali said "Don't wait for the world to recognize your greatness. Live it, and let the world catch up to you."

YOU are the master of your fate.

YOU are the captain of your soul.

2. As A Man Thinketh

Your thoughts have an enormous influence on your life. The quality of your life depends on the quality of your thoughts, so think well! You tend to become what you think. Better living begins with better thinking. What you tell yourself everyday will either lift you up or tear you down. Henry Ford said, "Whether you think you can or think you can't, you're right."

This chapter was influenced by a book of the same title by James Allen, written in 1903. Influenced himself by a verse in the Bible from the Book of Proverbs, chapter 23, verse 7: "As a man thinketh in his heart, so is he"; Allen was described as dealing with the power of thought, and particularly with the use and application of thought to happy and beautiful issues. It shows how, in his own thought-world, each man holds the key to every condition, good or bad, that enters into his life, and that, by working patiently and intelligently upon his thoughts, he may remake his life, and transform his circumstances. It was also described by Allen as "A book that will help you to help yourself", "A pocket companion for thoughtful people", and "A book on the power and right application of thought."

It was quoted by Buddha that "since everything is a reflection of our minds, everything can be changed by our minds." You have the ultimate power to direct your path in life by utilizing the strongest resource that human beings possess; our thoughts.

In one of my favorite books, Think and Grow Rich by Napoleon Hill, there was a poem that really hit home.

It emphasized what is known as the law of auto-suggestion; which suggests that your thoughts will lift you up or pull you down, according to the way you set your sails of THOUGHT.

*"If you think you are beaten, you are,
If you think you dare not, you don't
If you like to win, but think you can't,
It is almost certain you won't."*

*"If you think you'll lose, you're lost
For out of the world we find
Success begins with a fellow's will-
It's all in the state of mind."*

*"If you think you are outclassed, you are,
You've got to think high to rise,
You've got to be sure of yourself before
You can ever win a prize."*

*"Life's battles don't always go
To the stronger or faster man,
But soon or late the man who wins
Is the man WHO THINKS HE CAN!"*

In my opinion, most people's biggest fault is that they don't realize how great they are. Once you do that, your entire world changes. A paradigm shift has to take place. A fundamental change in thinking has to happen.

Give me a moment to share with you a concept on how you can reprogram your mindset and/or thinking patterns. One of my mentors, Gerry Robert, introduced me to the Captain and Crew concept which comes from his book The Millionaire Mindset, and is based on the premise that you/your conscious mind are the "CAPTAIN" and your subconscious mind is the "CREW." The subconscious mind listens to the instructions

2. As A Man Thinketh

given by the conscious mind, and obediently brings the instructions into reality. Whatever you say or think, your Crew will receive it as a command and respond, "YES, Captain!! Okay," and take it as an order. So be careful about what you say and think. "I'm so tired," or "You're driving me nuts," or "I never get anything done," or "This is very hard for me to do," or "I just can't seem to wrap my head around it," and other seemingly innocent thoughts will manifest as your Crew goes to work to make them true; all because the Captain said so.

One important thing to note is the Crew is not capable of formulating its own thinking. If the Captain fails to give specific instruction to the Crew, the Crew will just take ANY instruction passed to it and bring it to reality. So, what I want to emphasize here is the fact that you (the Captain) have within you the power to create anything you want, and the storehouse of this power is your subconscious mind (the Crew).

Dr. Richard Wiseman, author of The Luck Factor, said that some people appear to be evidently lucky, as if fortune specially favors them to make them satisfied and happy. But some others are trapped in the 'web of bad luck'. They face repeated failures, resulting in misfortune and sadness. We usually ascribe the luck factor to the governing stars or the law of karma. Can we really do anything to improve our luck?

Professor Wiseman spent over a decade studying people's attitude to luck and how they affect reality. His revolutionary study of luck and 'unluck' factors resulted in his bestselling book, The Luck Factor which has transformed the lives of many.

The difference between lucky and unlucky people is striking. Lucky people tend to imagine spontaneously even amidst severe misfortune. They keep their expectations quite high and continue to live in happiness merely by thinking and behaving like a lucky person. It may sound incredible but it is true.

The unlucky people are usually pessimistic and always sad. They attract negative situations and misfortunes with constant sadness, doubt and fear of failure.

Wiseman identified four basic principles that lucky persons knowingly or unknowingly followed. He explained these principles to the volunteers associated with his research picked from different age groups and advised them to follow the principles for a month. The result was dramatic. Unlucky people started attracting fortune and became really happy with firm belief system and corresponding behavior.

The tips are fairly simple. Listen to your instincts or gut feelings before taking any decision. They are usually right. Be open to new experiences and break the normal routine. Spend some time every day to remember what went well.

In closing, I leave you with these few facts. A man is literally what he thinks, his character being the complete sum of all his thoughts. We do not attract what we want, but what we are. Every action and feeling is preceded by a thought. Thinking is one of the strongest and most useful powers you possess. This power consists of your thoughts. The thoughts that pass through your mind are responsible for everything that happens in your life. Your predominant way of thinking influence your behavior and attitude and control your actions and reactions. You become the result of your thinking.

INVICTUS

Out of the night that covers me,
Black as the pit from pole to pole,
I thank whatever gods may be
For my unconquerable soul.

In the fell clutch of circumstance
I have not winced nor cried aloud.
Under the bludgeonings of chance
My head is bloody, but unbowed.

Beyond this place of wrath and tears
Looms but the Horror of the shade,
And yet the menace of the years
Finds and shall find me unafraid.

It matters not how strait the gate,
How charged with punishments the scroll,
I am the master of my fate,
I am the captain of my soul.

William Ernest Henley

3. The Showroom Car

It was between the years of 1993-1996, I would have particular conversations with a peculiar, old man. He was an extraordinary character. Some would say unsavory because of his previous occupation and the condition he was in at that time. Life had taken him on a whirlwind rollercoaster that brought him to South Dallas, and I was fortunate enough for him to land in my neighborhood. His name was Chicago Red. His past occupation was a pimp. Yes, that's right; I said a pimp. At the time, he was out of the game and making the best of his last days. There were many times that I would join him on the porch at a mutual meeting spot that we had. We would just talk. I was fascinated by the stories he would tell, and how clear and colorful he would paint a picture with his words.

In particular, one of the stories I loved the most was about "The Showroom Car on the Showroom Floor". I loved it so much, that I used to ask him to tell it to me again and again. It was a powerful message to me, and has guided me all my adult life. The story is about a man or woman having pride and self-respect; and to act accordingly. The story goes as such…….

When a person decides that they want to buy a new car, they go to the showroom floor and look at the car there. It is top-notch!! It has all of the bells and whistles, dings and dongs, so on and so on. Everyone wants that one. But typically, that one is not for sale. He said, "but there are a lot of look-a-likes outside on the lot"; so most people end up settling for the look-a-like. Not to say that there is anything wrong with that one, it's just not the one on the showroom floor. He would say "look here lil' brother, I need you to see what I'm saying"; while holding his hands up to his eyes like binoculars. "You have to carry yourself like the car on the showroom floor!! That car has pride and respect attached to it. It's not for everybody. Sure people can sit in it, look around, hell….even blow the horn!! But no one, and I mean no one is given the keys to start it." Then he would further explain that the reason that no one gets the keys is because if they get the key, they can put it in the ignition. When in the ignition, they can start the car. Once the car is started and the engine is running, it can be put in gear. Once in gear, it can be driven. Then he would ask me, "What is a new car once you drive it off the lot?!"…."USED!!! That's what it becomes…..so look a here", as Red would say.

"You have to have enough pride and respect for yourself and avoid giving the wrong people the key to put in your back and crank you up. Because once they crank you up, they can put you in gear. Once they have you in gear, they can drive you. Once they drive you, guess what…..YOU'RE USED!!!"

Chicago Red would go on and explain how people are just like cars. You have gently used cars that may have had one owner, and was well taken care of; and would make a great acquisition for the next person. You also have cars that have been treated very badly. They have had many wrecks, they have high mileage on them, etc. But the person selling the car would try and hide all the damage to the body, motor or interior in a way that you don't see it initially; just to get you to love it and buy it.

I could write an entire book on my conversations with Chicago Red, but I'll close this chapter with the moral of the story. In order to get to the next level of success, you must have pride in yourself. You must respect yourself enough to make the right decisions to put you in the right places, avoid the wrong places; and more importantly protect your value. Knowing your personal value will force you to make life's

3. The Showroom Car

decisions based on just that; your value. If you don't think much of yourself, your decisions will reflect it. If your self-esteem is low, your decisions will reflect it. If you think very highly of yourself, your decisions will reflect it.

I would love to go on and on about my conversations with my good friend, Chicago Red [may his soul rest in peace], but I will end with this.

Hold yourself in high regard, and the world will follow suit.

I promise myself

To be so strong that nothing can disturb my peace of mind.
To talk health, happiness, and prosperity to every person I meet.
To make all my friends feel that there is something worthwhile in them.
To look at the sunny side of everything and make my optimism come true.
To think only of the best, to work only for the best
and to expect only the best.
To be just as enthusiastic about the success of
others as I am about my own.
To forget the mistakes of the past and press on to the
greater achievements of the future.
To wear a cheerful expression at all times and give a smile
to every living creature I meet.
To give so much time to improving myself that I
have no time to criticize others.
To be too large for worry, too noble for anger, too strong for fear,
and too happy to permit the presence of trouble.
To think well of myself and to proclaim this fact to the world,
not in loud words, but in great deeds.
To live in the faith that the whole world is on my side,
so long as I am true to the best that is in me.

CHRISTIAN D. LARSON

4. Try & Let Go

Most people are just two habits away from the next level of success. One they must start, and one they must stop. In this chapter, I want to share with you two of the most important actions in life that I have discovered; To Try and To Let Go.

The majority of the people in the world will never experience greatness because they will not try to. When a man says I cannot, he has made a suggestion to himself that he is not capable. He has weakened his power of accomplishing that which otherwise would have been accomplished. One of the greatest motivational speakers in the world, Les Brown, said this…"You don't have to be great to get started, but you have to get started to be great." That statement should resonate with you and everyone else in the world. Imagine that. Greatness awaits you, only if you try to obtain it. I know and believe that every accomplishment begins with the decision to try. Once you have in your heart that you want to do something, and you have made it a goal that you have a burning desire to achieve; the only thing left for you to do is TRY.

One of my best friends and fellow author, Sugar Ray Destin, Jr. says in his book *Claim Your Destiny!*,"Don't follow your dreams. Chase them!" He said that you must make the declaration to chase your dreams with everything in your heart. The chase begins with you trying.

I saw this picture one day. It was a lady that looked as if she was training or working out. She was standing at the bottom of an enormous flight of stairs. It seemed to have extended to the top of the sky. The flight of stairs looked like it was parting the clouds as Moses parted the Red Sea. There was a message for the lady, etched in stone, at the bottom of the stairs. Before I go to the next important action in life, I want to share that simple message with you.

The message said, "There is no triumph without trying. All it takes is a little umph!!"

Let that marinate in your soul for a bit.

(Try + Umph = TRIUMPH)

LET GO!! That's the second important action in life I want to share with you. Sometimes in life, you will find yourself trying to hold on to certain things. Not realizing that if your hands are full with something that may not be serving your best interest, you will not be able to receive the thing that can and will. Holding on to something dead that needs to be let go of in order to free your hands up to receive the next blessing is very detrimental to your personal success and forward progress.

I grew up listening to and learning from the music that my parents played around the house when I was a kid. In 1978, there was this song that came out, that I really loved by L.T.D. featuring Jeffrey Osborne titled *Concentrate On You*. In the song, he made a statement that for some odd reason I really gravitated to as a kid. Maybe it was the melody. Maybe it was me receiving a message early in life. He sang, *"It takes separation to bring appreciation."* That was really the only part of the song I would sing over, and over again. At that time, of course, I didn't totally understand the weight of those words. As an adult, I fully understand and appreciate that statement. In life, we are going to have to separate from certain people, places, and things in order to discover and then appreciate the new opportunities that await us.

4. Try & Let Go

Not being able to let go will have us finding ourselves in some unwarranted predicaments. I want to share a parable with you. It's about the tale of the hunter, the monkey, and the peanuts.

There's a tale about how certain hunters in Africa catch monkeys. It can be very difficult to corral these intelligent creatures, so hunters have used a more inventive method…trapping a monkey by enticing him. A small jar is placed at the base of a tree with peanuts which may attract the monkey's curiosity.

The opening of the jar allows the monkey to place his hand in, but when he tries to withdraw it, he is unable to do so without letting go of the contents of the jar. Believe it or not, some monkeys will stay there with their hand in the jar until the hunter comes back to trap them!

It's not just monkeys who get trapped by what they are unwilling to let go of. We are guilty of the same. While, most of us would not be tempted by peanuts in a jar, it's amazing the things we will hang onto rather than let go of so we can move on. We get trapped because we are unwilling to let go of something we have, want, or are doing which is working against us.

To Try and To Let Go will introduce you to so many opportunities that life has to offer. As the famous Nike slogan instructs us to, *"Just Do It."*

Try & Let Go.

"There is nothing
outside of yourself
that can ever enable you
to get better, stronger, richer,
quicker, or smarter.
Everything is within.
Everything exists.
Seek nothing
outside of yourself."

- Miyamoto Musashi

5. Is That For Me?

Sometimes we face the challenges of trying to decide who and what we are responsible for. First, and foremost, we must know, accept, embrace and demonstrate that we are responsible for ourselves. A good number of people have asked me who am I writing the book for or why did I write the book. Simply, my answer was me. This book is written for me. It is to hold me accountable for the knowledge acquired over the years through school and life experiences. The book was published so that I may share it with the world.

Many have said that knowledge is power. I beg to differ. The application of knowledge is power. I know of many educated fools. Why fools?....because they have the knowledge and won't apply it. I've been a fool before. That's how I know, and why I can say that.

Once you have knowledge, you become responsible for that which you possess. Responsibility has been defined as the ability to act independently and make decisions without authorization; the state or fact of being accountable for something; and the state or fact of having a duty to deal with something or of having control over someone. I like to add to the definition by saying that one is "RESPONSE-ABLE". You are able to respond because of the knowledge you possess.

Many times, we run from things that we feel are not for us; when in reality, it belongs to us. We feel certain things are not our responsibility because it doesn't directly affect us. Depending on your knowledge, you are held accountable for certain things. It may be personal, shared, or even social responsibilities.

You must have and develop the confidence to face the challenges in life that *are for you*. Success builds that confidence. When I say "are for you", I'm not just talking about your personal challenges. You may be responsible for being a leader in a situation because of your knowledge of a subject matter. If you fail to step up and address that challenge, then you have failed yourself and those affected by the situation. You could have provided the clarity, leadership, or understanding needed to move that challenge forward in a positive manner.

It is your duty as a human being to become a part of the solution. I used to have some business cards with P.P.S. behind my name. It stood for Professional Problem Solver. One of the guarantees in life is that there will always be a problem. It's said that the best way to stay employed is to always have a solution for a problem. Becoming a solutions provider puts you in the mindset of being ready to face life's challenges, and not run from them as if they don't belong to you.

When I decided to name this chapter Is That For Me?, I did it with the purpose in mind of having the reader ask themselves that question when faced with an obstacle in life. I want to challenge the reader to honestly assess their knowledge and begin to apply it when facing a problem. If you possess the solution for a problem through the application of your knowledge, then it is your duty to accept responsibility for that matter.

Leaders and winners are all the same. We step up and face life's challenges head on because we embrace the fact that our knowledge is our advantage and protection. It gives us the power to be responsible and apply that knowledge in order to become a solutions provider for ourselves and others.

5. Is That For Me?

We are excited about every opportunity to ask ourselves the question, *"Is That For Me?"*

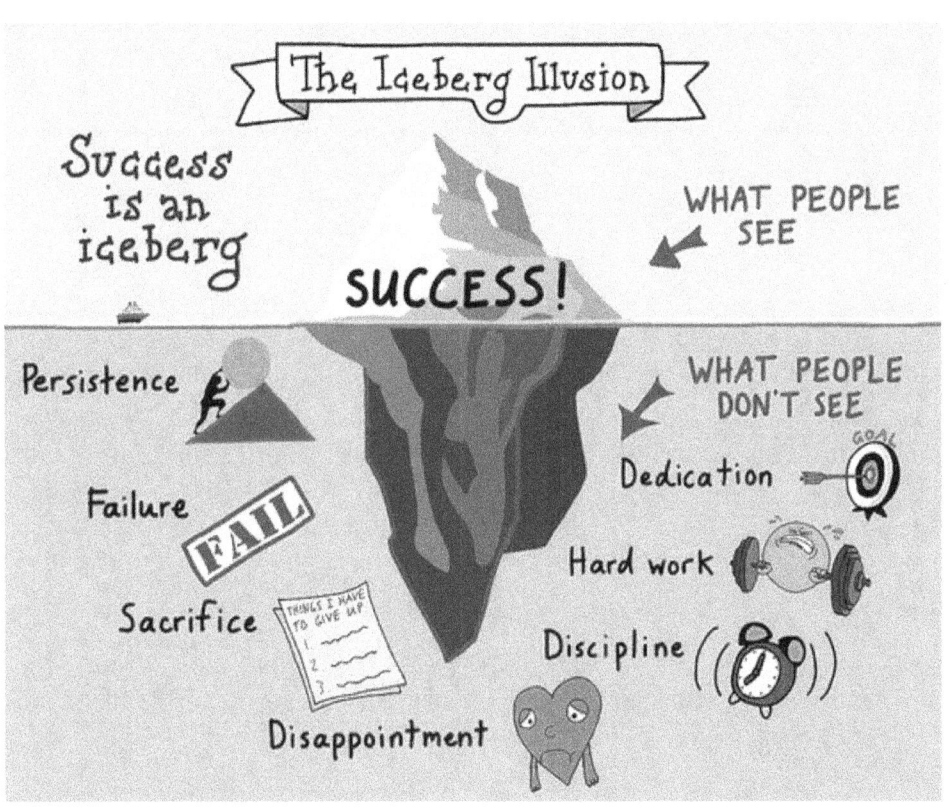

6. Check Your Expectations

We have all heard the statement "mind over matter." If you don't mind, it doesn't matter. Let's examine that for a minute. To me, that statement says that if I don't care much about the outcome of a situation; then I won't let it bother me. I like to check my expectations sometimes by saying to myself that if it will not matter 5 days from now, 5 weeks from now, or 5 years from now; then it doesn't matter now.

That method of thinking allows me to release situations that could become toxic if I give too much credibility to them. If I, you, or we continue to give credit to or not expect toxic people or situations to be just that; then we will forever set ourselves up for frustrations.

I believe and preach that *your frustrations come from your expectations*. For instance, if I'm expecting you to meet me at 3:30pm and you show up at 4:00pm; chances are that I will end up being frustrated with you. If I check my expectations and tell you to meet me at 3:00pm, knowing you may be late and show up at 3:30pm then I've prevented myself from being disappointed and frustrated by you.

Many times people unknowingly expect certain things from people or situations. When the thing that they expected doesn't happen, the frustration sets in. When I say "Check Your Expectations", I'm simply saying mentally prepare yourself for the worst. Know that there is a possibility that the worst is bound to happen in any situation or by any person; and plan accordingly. I'm not saying not to have faith in people; but I am saying be totally realistic. Plan for the bad, just as well as you plan for the good.

When you learn to keep your expectations in check, you develop an enormous power over any frustrations that could possibly occur. It is important to avoid unnecessary frustrations because they can become a hindrance and derail you from your daily process to success.

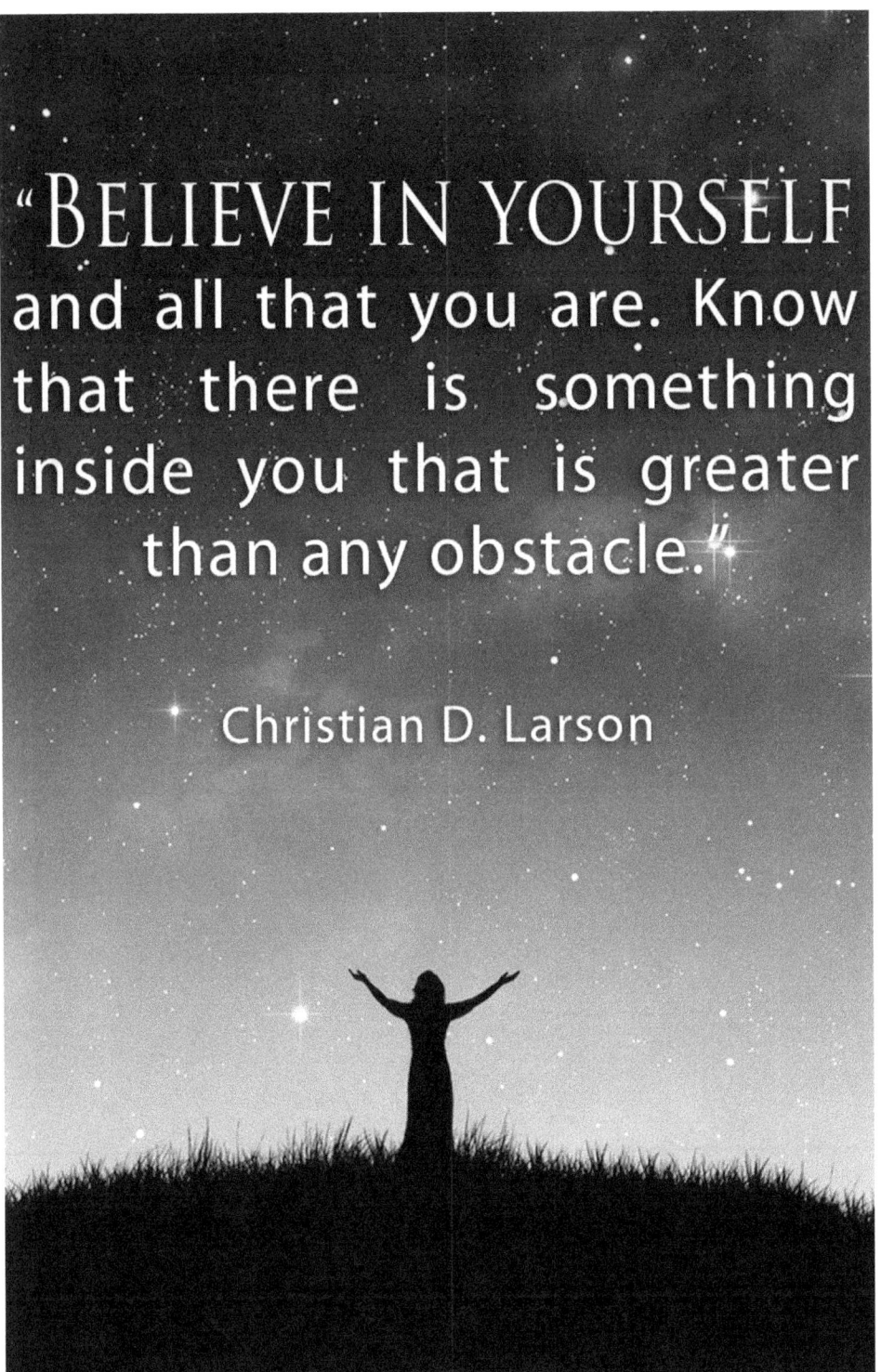

7. Perception Is Reality

The way you perceive things are based on your interpretation of your life experiences; thus your reality. Your interpretation of your life experiences is influenced by your belief system. What we believe is the way we think, and the way we think is what we see.

Take me for example, I'm an optimist. I always see the glass as half full versus it being half empty. I'm always looking for the positive side of things. So to me, the glass is really half full. Meaning that just a little more is needed, and the glass will be full. A pessimist would say that the glass is half empty, only seeing the negative side. Either way, we are both correct. Our individual perceptions create our individual realities.

A good friend of mine, Jon Dixon, said "beliefs are everything, and they shape your perception." I always told him that I wanted to add to that by pointing out that someone's life experiences will also shape their perception. So we agreed that the experiences make way for the beliefs.

It is said that humans tend to form beliefs without realizing that sometimes these beliefs skew reality for us. We build into these beliefs an explanation that favors ourselves. Then those beliefs are what we rely on to react to the world. In fact, those beliefs cause us to have the emotion that we have. If you are sad about a situation, it only means that you believe that the situation is a sad one. Someone else may have a different perspective that is generated from their unique set of beliefs.

One of my favorite quotes is something that Albert Einstein said….."Everything is energy and that's all there is to it. Match the frequency of the reality you want and you cannot help but get that reality. It can be no other way. This is not philosophy. This is physics." The frequency at which we vibrate is determined by the beliefs that we buy into. It is how we interpret the world and how we react to the world.

The law of attraction says that "we create our own reality." We do that because of our beliefs. If you believe that success is for you to have, then you will begin to act on that belief. You will begin to see things from the vantage point of success being something that you can obtain. It becomes real to you. Your every thought and coinciding action now puts you on the course to becoming successful. Your perception became your reality.

However you perceive something to be, you have just chosen your reality with regards to that matter. You can truthfully be having a very bad day, but depending on how you choose to see it; your attitude and entire day can change. My life consists of peaks and valleys. When I'm in the valley, I'm looking to get to the next peak. When I'm at a peak, I'm appreciating, cherishing, and trying to maintain my "peak position". I could easily say, "woe is me", and let the fact that I'm deep in the valley cause me to produce a negative perception of where I am. Or, as I do….I say that there is nowhere to go but up from here. And with that perception, I become encouraged by the fact that I know that the peak awaits me.

Take a moment and look at the illustration on the next page. Tell me what you see…………Do you see a beautiful woman dressed to perfection, ready for an awesome evening out with a very nice, fashionable, fur shawl over her shoulders? Or do you see a sad, elderly woman with a big nose, wearing a bonnet, possibly in the cold, dreary night?

7. Perception Is Reality

This image shows that two people can see the same thing, disagree, and yet both are right. It's not logical; it's psychological. In The Seven Habits of Highly Effective People, Stephen Covey uses this image in a perception demonstration. He goes into great detail about how conditioning affects our perceptions. It shows that paradigms are the source of our attitudes and behaviors. He said, "Each of us tends to think we see things as they are, and that we are objective. But this is not the case. We see the world, not as it is, but as we are — or, as we are conditioned to see it."

Based on what your life experiences have conditioned you to see, your perception will be influenced by that.

LUCKY BY CHOICE

Your perception in life can also be determined by where you stand in life. In the illustration above, there is a debate on whether there is a 6 or 9 on the ground. Whatever the reasoning from either gentleman, they are both correct; because of the position each is standing in.

Understanding conditioning and influences (whether it be life experiences, location, family, friends, school, work, or any number of social components) will help you in recognizing why one would perceive something the way they do. It in turn allows you to interact more effectively because you understand why their perception is their reality.

8. I Can't Sleep

Have you ever been so anxious about something that you couldn't go to sleep? You know, like when you were younger and you couldn't wait until the first day of school. You would lay your school clothes out and get everything in order, all in super anticipation of what the day will bring. What about on Christmas Eve? Your parents tell you to go to sleep so that you can wake up in the morning and open your gifts on Christmas day. Well, that's how I am about my goals and dreams!!

I can't sleep sometimes because my dreams keep me awake. I get so excited about working on my goals that as I lay there in my bed, it becomes difficult to fall asleep. I begin to think about the things that need to be done, and the excitement and achievement that it will bring. I even keep a notepad next to my bed, so that as I come up with ideas and strategies, I can write them down. It's just something about writing it down in my own handwriting that gets me wired up.

Napoleon Hill, the author of the classic book "Think and Grow Rich", spoke about having a burning desire to accomplish your dreams. He said, "there is one quality which one must possess to win, and that is definiteness of purpose, the knowledge of what one wants, and a burning desire to possess it." That burning desire is the starting point for all human achievement.

My burning desire to win at life and succeed at accomplishing my dreams is what keeps my mind wide awake.

LUCKY BY CHOICE

I'm pretty sure you have many dreams that are waiting to be realized. Don't put limits on yourself. Don't be afraid to dream big.

I would like to share an excerpt from one of my speeches with you. I was inspired by Danny Aiello's monologue in the movie "The Closer" when I wrote it. In the case you don't get to see me speak in person anytime soon, I at least want to leave you with this……..

"People ask me what it took to get where I am today.
What it takes to reach this level of success.
I say sacrifice……. We make heroes of ourselves in the name of sacrifice. What we are willing to give up in the pursuit of a dream. What we are willing to pay. Who we are willing to lose. There is no success without sacrifice. There are no obstacles you can't overcome.
There is nothing between you and your goals.
So stop cheating yourself, and go after what you want.
If you succeed on your own terms, you don't owe anybody any explanations. But if you fail on their terms, you've got
a whole lot of explaining to do.
A man doesn't strive for greatness and embrace mediocrity.
That's called compromising.
There is no compromise in a dream. Compromising is an excuse for falling short while you lay on your couch with your smart phone scrolling on social media, or in front of your TV with your remote control, and a glass of whatever you are drinking….while you watch somebody else run with your dream. THAT'S YOUR DREAM!!
YOU HAVE TO GET UP AND GO GET IT!!
So do me this favor. Don't wake up one morning when your hair is grey, the elastic is gone out of your waistline, your clothes don't fit the same, and you got this funny look all over your face, and you look in that mirror…and you ask yourself….what the hell have I been doing for the last 10,20,30 years.
And then you say to yourself, this isn't my life.
This isn't where my passion lies.

8. I Can't Sleep

Well guess what…..before that happens, you've got to do something!!! Don't be afraid of your ambitions. If your dreams don't scare you, then they are not big enough!!! Nothing great ever came from a comfort zone.
If you blame other people for holding you back, then you're the problem and you don't want it bad enough….and don't tell me you do. Because other people don't stop you from dreaming,
YOU STOP YOU FROM DREAMING!!!
You get in your own way, because you're afraid of what you might become.
Even if that something is a wonderful, awesome, phenomenal thing.
Luck isn't some mystical energy that dances around the universe randomly bestowing people with satisfaction and joy.
You create your own luck.
It's a choice you have to make.
Luck won't choose you. You have to choose it.
The Choice Is Yours!!"

I hope that me sharing that excerpt with you motivates you to go after your dreams. Chase them with the burning desire that you possess for your own personal success.

In closing, I want to encourage you to use your imagination. Visualize the success that you want for yourself. Picture yourself doing all of the things that you wish to do in life. Don't defer your dreams any longer. I know sometimes we may have some beautiful nightmares called "mistakes" along the way. Just don't lose sight of your vision, goals, and dreams. Success is a wake up away. Sweet dreams.

DON'T FEAR FAILURE. FEAR BEING IN THE EXACT SAME PLACE NEXT YEAR AS YOU ARE TODAY.

9. Purpose & Reason

Mark Twain said, "The two most important days in your life are the day you are born, and the day you find out why." In this chapter, I will briefly highlight some solid philosophy behind the beliefs of purpose and reason.

Purpose has been defined as the reason for which something is done or created or for which something exists. Although purpose and reason are sometimes considered synonyms, I believe there is a slight difference in them. In my opinion, your purpose is the what and your reason is the why. The purpose is the goal and the reason is the inspiration, and why you reach the goal.

Your purpose will dictate what you will do with your life, and your reason will always explain why. For example, my purpose in life is to be a humble, servant leader and bridge-builder. My reason is to leave a legacy that will benefit my family, friends, associates, and all that will come after me. Your purpose will be full of passion. It will be that thing that comes automatic to you; the thing that you love doing the most. Sometimes you will hear people say that it's their "calling". If you have a strong purpose in life, you don't have to be pushed. Your passion will drive you there.

Living on purpose is the only way to really live. Everything else is only existing. The purpose of life is not only to be happy. It is to be useful, to be honorable, to be compassionate; to have it make some difference that you have lived and lived well. Be brave enough to live the life of your dreams according to your purpose instead of the expectations and opinions of others. Nothing is more creative... nor destructive... than a brilliant mind with a purpose. You can have anything you want if you want it badly enough. You can be anything you want to be, do anything you set out to accomplish if you hold to that desire with the singleness of purpose.

What is your why? What is your reason for living? Your REASON is your WHY!!

Finding your reason why is essential if you want to achieve success. If you don't have a strong reason behind your actions, your actions are less likely to create quality results. If you do have a strong "why" you have all the fuel you need to drive you forward – to success.

When you wake up every morning – What drives you?

If you want to live a life of complete success, happiness and fulfillment, you must find your reason. If you don't know what your reason is; if you don't know what drives you; what inspires you; then you have no reason to improve your life. How can you improve your life if you have no reason to improve it?

Why are you different from everyone else that's trying to do the same thing you're doing? What makes you stand out? Why are you so important!? Your reason will pull you up when you feel like you don't have the strength to get up anymore. Your reason will keep you fighting when everyone else thinks you are out for the count.

If you have not done so yet, I challenge you to take an assessment of yourself. Ask yourself two questions. What is my purpose? What is my reason? Take your time and make sure you get it right. The answers to both questions will be directly connected to your heart's desires in life. Once you have those

9. Purpose & Reason

answers, write them down. Turn them into your goals. Plan out how you will fulfill your purpose in life, and your reasons will drive you every step of the way.

10. Beyond The Basics

A man doesn't strive for greatness and embrace mediocrity.

I will be very brief in this chapter, because a lot does not have to be said. There's a saying that I use a lot….."what's understood doesn't have to be explained." So I'm not going to waste my time or yours trying to explain something to you that you already know. Instead, I will just remind you of a few things. Before I remind you, I have a story I want to share with you.

I can remember one night at a step show in Huntsville, Texas at Sam Houston State University in 1997. It was actually at the Walker County Fairgrounds. My team, the Bloody Rho Theta Chapter of Omega Psi Phi Fraternity from Prairie View A&M University, came in prepared. I was what we call "the march master", the leader of the march team (step team). We were full of enthusiasm, precision, and by far the best performance that night. We were easily the crowd favorite. After all the teams performed, the judges totaled the scores and came back with their decision. We received 2nd place!!! Can you believe that!!!! 2nd place!!! Now here comes the twist. Displaying good sportsmanship, we went on stage as a team and accepted the 2nd place trophy. Immediately after, I went out back and "slung" the trophy high in the sky, as far away from me as possible, in a dark open field. The people that saw me do that was confused, and immediately certified me as crazy. They thought that I should have been happy. My answer to them was that "2nd place is the first loser!!....2nd place is mediocre!!!" Now of course they looked at me like a sore loser. But I'm not. I'm just not into being rewarded for not winning. That's what mediocrity is made of. In the words of Ricky Bobby in the movie *Talladega Nights*...."If you're not first...you're last!!!"

If you want to succeed in life, you need to internalize this idea of excellence. Not many folks spend a lot of time trying to be excellent. Learn to break out of patterns of mediocrity. Become an expert at the basics....that's the only way you can move above mediocrity. You can't spend too much time on what should be the elementary things. DON'T MAJOR IN MINOR THINGS!!

The fear of being average motivates me. I strive to get the maximum out of the minimum. In a book titled "The Power of Broke" by Daymond John, he explained how having less created more. He said that desperation breeds innovation. When you have the will to win, a heart full of hope, and a ferocious drive to succeed by any means possible.....then you will rise above being average and mediocre. He said that a place of desperation, hope, and hunger forces you to think more creatively. It forces you to use your resources more efficiently. It forces you to be true to yourself, stay laser focused on your goals, and come up with innovative solutions required to succeed.

Keep in mind these things........Your attitude determines your altitude. The only real limitation on your abilities is the level of your desires. If you want to reach a higher level of success badly enough, there are no limits on what you can achieve. Listen to your instincts or gut feelings before taking any decision. They are usually right. Be open to new experiences and break the normal routine. Step out of your comfort zone. Greatness doesn't live there. Spend some time every day to remember what went well so that you can use that as a foundation and continue to build upon it.

10. Beyond The Basics

Lastly, the bottom is overcrowded. Rise to the top. If you have to succeed to survive, you will.

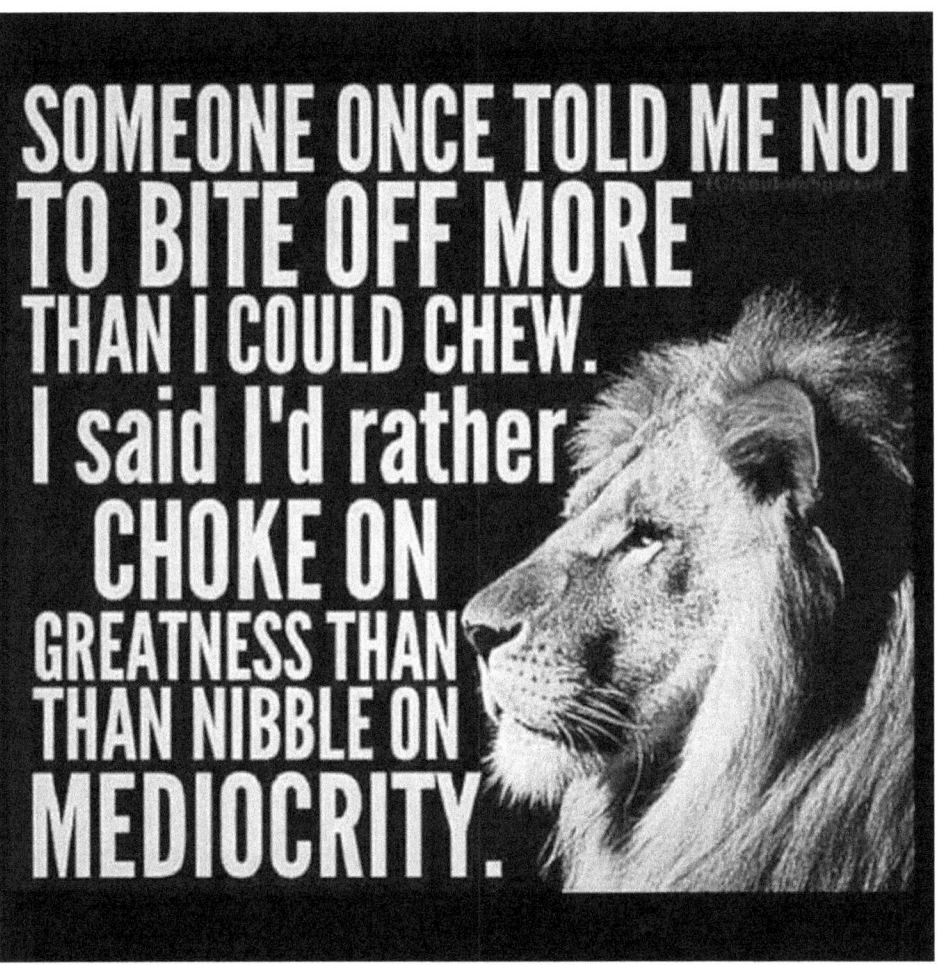

11. Birds Of A Feather

I know everyone has heard the age old saying that birds of a feather flock together. It's an old proverb that basically says people of the same sort or with the same tastes and interests will be found together. Let's paint this picture…..chickens flock with chickens, pigeons flock with pigeons, crows flock with crows, and so on.

Who are you flocking with?

The people we surround ourselves with either raise or lower our standards. They either help us to become the best version of ourselves or encourage us to become lesser versions of ourselves. We become like our friends. No man becomes great on his own. No woman becomes great on her own. The people around them help to make them great. We all need people in our lives that will raise our standard, remind us of our essential purpose, and challenge us to become the best version of ourselves.

If you want to know your future, show me your friends. The people around you are directly connected to your destiny.

Take the average income of the 5 people closest to you; most likely, your income will be 10% less or more than the average of those people. You are the sum total of the 5 people you mostly associate with. That is your circle of success. The power of influence and the concept of success through association are very, very real paradigms. Your network becomes your net worth.

LUCKY BY CHOICE

On the flip side, you may have people around you that mean you no good. If so, you need to change your flock. They may be in your circle, but not in your corner. You must surround yourself with people that fill in the gaps of your weaknesses, not perpetuate or exploit your weaknesses. You must bring value to the flock as well.

You will sometimes outgrow your friends. I want to share a personal story with you about a pair of pants I had when I was a kid. At that time, they were my favorite pair of pants. They were some dark drown corduroy pants with perfect pockets, perfect pleats, the right length, etc. I mean everything about those pants were perfect to me. Eventually, I couldn't wear the pants anymore. There was nothing wrong with the pants. There was nothing wrong with me. I simply outgrew the pants.

On your journey to success, you WILL outgrow people, places, and things. Some will even have been your favorite at a certain time in your life.

When those pants were my favorite, I was around 7 or 8 years old. Imagine me trying to squeeze into those pants today as a 40 year old man. I would look quite foolish right...LOL!!! Just for even attempting to put them on, would make the craziest person look at me like I'm crazy. Well, that's what happens when we try to hold on to the people, places, and things that we outgrow in life. Trust and believe me when I say, it's okay. There is nothing wrong with you. There is nothing wrong with them. You're simply outgrowing old things that don't fit you anymore.

Your successful elevation may require separation and isolation. You may be flocking as a chicken right now, but if you want to soar like an eagle, you will have to remove yourself from the chicken coup. Sure, you will leave those

11. Birds Of A Feather

friendly feathers behind. There's nothing wrong with that, and you don't have to feel guilty about it. When you begin to separate from your friends and rise above the rest; remember this. You don't have to slow down or go back down to bring them along. If they want to experience the success that you are, they have to do what you've done, elevate, separate, isolate, and catch up to you.

My last bit of advice to you is to always evaluate the people in your life; then promote, demote, or terminate them. You're the CEO of your life.

NO magic potions
No fairy dust
No one to do
it for You...
Just Me,
I will push YOU,
show YOU how
to put one determined foot
in front of the other.
That's what I will do.
I am INSIDE YOU...
I'm called your
INNER STRENGTH.
Dig deep down and find me.

12. Who Do You Believe In?

You are the most influential person you will talk to everyday. Why? It's simple; because you are your first line of communication. You are your thoughts. Your thoughts become your action. Your action becomes your habits. Your habits become your character. Your character becomes your destiny. You are responsible for you. You are the master of your fate, and the captain of your soul.

You have to believe in you. You have to take orders from yourself. So that means you have to trust yourself more than anything in the world. If you don't know how, it is absolutely imperative that you learn, immediately.

Faith in yourself is the "eternal elixir" which gives life, power, and action to anything you think you ever want to accomplish in life. Believing in yourself will produce miracles. It doesn't matter who believes in you, as long as you believe in you. It's the lack of faith in themselves that makes people afraid of meeting challenges.

Belief in yourself will lead you to the next steps in life. If you are motivated by a mindset of self belief then you will be moving towards a greater life.

By now, it's no secret that I am really into music; more specifically, the lyrics. There have been many songs that describe self-belief and self confidence. There's one in particular that I want to talk about. "I Believe I Can Fly" by R. Kelly is without a doubt one of the best inspirational songs made, ever. The lyrics in the hook of the song gives you the right mindset to adopt as it pertains to self-belief.

LUCKY BY CHOICE

"I believe I can fly
I believe I can touch the sky
I think about it every night and day
Spread my wings and fly away
I believe I can soar
I see me running through that open door
I believe I can fly....."

In addition to that song, R. Kelly also wrote another chart-topping inspirational hit. "The World's Greatest" appears on the Ali soundtrack. It channels the never-ending self-confidence of today's professional artists and athletes, while employing the title deservedly given to Muhammad Ali.

Muhammad Ali was without a shadow of a doubt the most confident person most people have ever met or heard of. Ali believed in himself so much that he made jokes about it, when the whole time he was as serious as you could possible get. He once said, "I am the greatest. I said that even before I knew I was." He also said, "To be a great champion, you must believe you are the best. If you're not, pretend you are." Muhammad Ali understood the value and impact of self-belief and self-confidence. That belief was his fuel to propel him to the top as a champion in boxing, and in life.

Who do you believe in? Who do you think you are? I hope you believe and think you are and will continue to be your greatest self through self-discovery, self-assessment, self-improvement, self-empowerment, and self belief.

13. What's Your Story?

Everyone has a story to tell or one that will be told. Before getting deep into this chapter, I want to introduce you to a poem titled The Dash by Linda Ellis.

"I read of a man who stood to speak
at the funeral of a friend.
He referred to the dates on the tombstone
from the beginning…to the end.

He noted that first came the date of birth
and spoke the following date with tears,
but he said what mattered most of all
was the dash between those years.

For that dash represents all the time
that she spent alive on earth.
And now only those who loved her
know what that little line is worth.

For it matters not, how much we own,
the cars…the house…the cash.
What matters is how we live and love
and how we spend our dash.

So, think about this long and hard.
Are there things you'd like to change?
For you never know how much time is left
that can still be rearranged.

If we could just slow down enough
to consider what's true and real

LUCKY BY CHOICE

*and always try to understand
the way other people feel.*

*And be less quick to anger
and show appreciation more
and love the people in our lives
like we've never loved before.*

*If we treat each other with respect
and more often wear a smile,
remembering that this special dash
might only last a little while.*

*So, when your eulogy is being read,
with your life's actions to rehash...
would you be proud of the things they say
about how you spent YOUR dash?"*

So my question to you right now is; How will you spend your dash? That poem inspires me to continue to build upon my legacy, and prepare to leave something of value for my family, friends, associates, and all that will come after me.

In chapter 9, I discussed Purpose & Reason. I talked about "What Is Your Why?" I'm about to share a very personal moment with you, and will be very candid on how and where the moment was experienced.

In 1999, I was in federal prison in Seagoville, Texas. I had been there about 5 months on a 15 month sentence. I was making the best of a bad situation. One day, I was engaged in a very intellectual conversation with an older gentleman from South Africa named Richard. Richard was an old White man in his late 60's at the time. He said to me, "I like you, but Black

13. What's Your Story

people make me sick!!" Now mind you, because of where I am, you have to keep your head on a swivel and look very deep into why people say and do things. You never know what they are up to. So I asked why. He said, "because your people are selfish and don't do anything but leave bills and problems when they die." Now at this moment, he's ruffled a feather or two of mine, but I want to see where he's going with this. So I indulge him a bit more. Then it got deep.

He asked me, "do you know your great, great, great, great, great, great, great-grandfather?" I said "no." He said, "because that motherfucker didn't leave you anything!!" At that moment, old or not, I was ready to pulverize that old man for that statement. But for so many reasons, I knew I couldn't. He continued by saying, "I bet Martin Luther King, Jr.'s great, great, great, great, great, great, great-grandson knows who he is." He simply explained, "because he left him something."

That was an in your face, hard punch to the nose awakening. Of course that wasn't my first time hearing the word legacy, but it was definitely the first time it was delivered like that. I think the shock value of it all was what made it stick.

In that conversation, I found out "my why." My reason for living was made very clear. I realized that my life ain't about me. We went on to talk about the importance of leaving a legacy for your family. Leaving an inheritance for your children; leaving your family in a position of head start when you pass away. Richard told me to make sure that when I die that the quality of life for my family either stays the same or improves. He told me that you shouldn't be living your life for yourself, you should be living it for them.

Every decision I make now, I make for the future; and not just my future. I understand the importance of becoming a true bridge-builder for the next generations to come. I know that I must leave something of value. I must do something great in life to be remembered by.

I must leave a legacy.

Before I go, I want to challenge you to start building your legacy. Understand that your life's decisions have to be about more than your own selfish desires. You are building a story that the dash on your tombstone will represent. What will your story be? What will your legacy represent?

Keep this last bit of advice in mind…..

Your legacy is not only what people remember about you. It is what people will do differently because they met you.

Be Phenomenal or Be Forgotten.

Part Two:

EXECUTIVE DECISIONS

14. Thinking For A Change

Every now and then, something remarkable comes our way; something that revolutionizes the way we think. A paradigm shift happens; something that holds the key to drastically transform our lives from average to excellent.

A while back, I really believed that if it wasn't for bad luck, I wouldn't have any. I had foundational issues that needed to be addressed in order to correct some systemic damage that I caused, and allowed to happen to me.

Life began to introduce me to some major losses. I immediately recognized that I had to make some pivotal, integrity based decisions if I planned on overcoming those losses.

I could no longer just want or expect change. I had to think for a change. I had to literally guarantee that my way of thinking created change. I sat for a while, reflecting on everything that I knew that I was not applying to my life. I learned and knew that creation starts in the subconscious mind. I recognized that I had habits that influenced the paradigms in my life, which affected the programming of my process of creation.

The process of creation has 4 steps; beliefs, perspective, instructions, and actions. Almost every successful person begins with two beliefs: the future can be better than the present, and I have the power to make it so. The necessary perspective is influenced by the strength of the beliefs. At that point, we begin to give ourselves instructions to follow. Then, we take action.

When you can't see past a choice you don't understand, based on your way of thinking; that is the moment when you begin to make the wrong decisions.

In order to manage your thinking process, you must first learn, what you are responsible for and what you are not responsible for. In the thinking process, there are two kinds of thoughts; unconscious thoughts and conscious thoughts. An unconscious thought is one that you have, but are unaware of. Many times an unconscious thought can cause an emotion, and the only thing you are aware of, is the emotion you feel. There are two types of conscious thoughts, automatic thoughts and chosen thoughts. Sometimes, you have a thought that just occurs to you. That is an automatic thought. You are aware of it. You just didn't choose to think it. You just noticed that you had a thought, about someone or something. The second kind of conscious thought, is a chosen thought. This is a thought that you choose to think, usually in response to an automatic thought.

Now that you understand what makes up your thinking process, no you can manage it. More importantly, it's time to persuade your brain to think for a change.

15. G-14 Classified

Ships don't sink because of the water around them. Ships sink because of the water that gets in them. Don't let what's happening around you get inside you and weigh you down. Make sure everybody in your boat is rowing, and not drilling holes when you are not looking. This chapter is about protecting yourself from outside influences.

Now some of you may notice the chapter title "G-14 Classified" from the movie *Rush Hour* starring Chris Tucker and Jackie Chan. Funny right?!?! I loved the movie too; so much so that I titled the chapter from that scene in the movie.

Follow me on this. Even though in the movie, G-14 Classified is a made up term; I wanted to bring some life to it. See, in life you have to treat yourself like a highly classified case. Pay attention to the details. You must handle yourself with care. You may even consider yourself fragile.

There is a lot of advice that I want to share with you in this chapter, so instead of turning this chapter into a book in itself, I will give you a list of 9 self-explanatory statements:

1. Respect is non-negotiable. It's not up for grabs. Never compromise your self-respect.

2. Be careful who you tell about your dreams, because there are dream-killers in the world.

3. Protect your mental space, and evict negative energy.

4. Invest in people who you know will feed you just as much goodness as you do them.

5. Don't let people put their limitations on you.

6. Stop doing the most for people that won't do the least for you.

7. Don't set yourself on fire to keep the wrong people warm.

8. Build in silence, because people won't know what, when, how, and where to attack you until it's too late.

9. If you allow people to make more withdrawals than deposits in your life, you will be out of balance and in the negative. Know when to close the account.

They say an ounce of prevention is worth a pound of cure. Focus on protecting yourself in order to prevent any unwarranted or unnecessary damage to your mental state of being. There will be people that try and discourage you from doing certain things because they can't see themselves doing it. Don't let someone who quit on their dreams try to discourage you from following yours.

*Keep your thoughts positive
because your thoughts
become your words.*

*Keep your words positive
because your words
become your behavior.*

*Keep your behavior positive
because your behavior
becomes your habits.*

*Keep your habits positive
because your habits
become your values.*

*Keep your values positive
because your values
become your destiny.*

-Mahatma Gandhi

16. Tomorrow Never Comes

What is always coming, but never arrives?
TOMORROW.

This chapter is solely about procrastination and how to overcome it; and maximizing your day. Powerful speaker, Eric Thomas said, "There is no such thing as procrastination. Your priorities are out of order."

Put first things first. Prioritize. Don't put off for tomorrow, what can be done today.

When you want something bad enough you will make it your highest priority to make it happen. Get it done. Stop living on excuses! Maybe you just don't know what you want in life so it's hard to prioritize your goals the way that you should. Many can say they want a lot of materialistic possessions, money and such. But aside from a nice car, a nice house, being financially free and all that type of stuff…What do you really want out of life? Dig deeper within yourself and discover what your purpose is. Discover yourself and see what it is that YOU have to offer. How can you make a difference? This process will help order your priorities from least important to the most important events of your life.

But if you already know what you want in life and still can't seem to follow through. Then ask yourself, what is distracting me? Be honest, you owe it to yourself.

Is it because you are waiting on the right time? Stop waiting until the time is right, and realize the time is now. There is not always a right time, but there will always be a right now. You have to learn to take advantage of today, right now.

Is it because you are intimidated by the goal? Break it down into pieces. Inch by inch anything's a cinch. Yard by yard, life is hard.

Is it because you are waiting until you are ready? You can't let your quest for perfection hinder your process or progress. If you wait until you're perfect, you'll be waiting for the rest of your life!!

Develop a sense of urgency. Do It ASAP!! As a matter of fact, Digger Phelps (the winningest men's basketball coach in Notre Dame's storied athletic history) said, "Do it yesterday, because tomorrow might not come."

In 2004, I had a warrant issued for my arrest for probation violation. I knew if arrested, I was going to jail with no bond. So instead of turning myself in, I adjusted and prepared my life and daily routine to evade the law. I procrastinated, because I didn't want to face the inevitable. I came up with excuse after excuse on why I shouldn't turn myself in yet. Silly me, I told myself..."you just need to wait until you get everything in order, and go when it's the right time." That was my story, and I stuck with it. I remember going to see my attorney, Ricky Anderson; and told him the same thing. He told me the truest statement ever. He said, "Good Brother (he's my frat brother as well), There is no right time to go to jail!" At that time, that's not what I wanted to hear. So I did nothing about it. I kept on going, running, and hiding; inconveniencing myself and others. I was a fugitive for 7 years!!! It all came to an end on a Thursday evening in April 2011. On that day, I exhaled. Finally, I can get on with my life. I served a two year prison sentence in

16. Tomorrow Never Comes

the Texas Department of Criminal Justice. When you see me in person, I'll tell you all of the details!! Don't forget to ask.

That life lesson taught me to abandon procrastinating. It didn't serve me well. I learned that there isn't a right time, there is a right now. So now, I act accordingly.

I learned that procrastination had a domino and ripple effect. It just doesn't affect that one thing, it affected much more. It does so because procrastinating is not just a thing to do; it's a mindset; a bad habit that must be erased.

As I finish my thoughts on this matter, I want to encourage you to maximize and to take advantage of the gift of today; unwrap it. Every day you are handed 86,400 seconds of endless possibilities; 1,440 minutes to make progress towards your goals; 24 golden hours to step into your greatness.

Yesterday is history. Tomorrow is a mystery. Today is a gift. That's why it's called the present.

Today is the tomorrow you worried about yesterday. No more procrastinating. The time is right now!!

"The best way to predict the future is to create it."

— PETER DRUCKER

17. Change Your Words, Change Your World

The power of words is magnificent!! Words bring life to dead situations. Words are singularly the most powerful force available to humanity. We can choose to use this force constructively with words of encouragement, or destructively using words of despair. Words have energy and power with the ability to help, to heal, to hinder, to hurt, to harm, to humiliate and to humble.

What will you do with that power? You have the uncanny ability to speak anything into existence.

Words are not simply sounds caused by air passing through our larynx. Words have real power. Words do more than convey information. The power of our words can actually destroy one's spirit; even stir up hatred and violence. They not only exacerbate wounds but inflict them directly. Of all the creatures on this planet, only man has the ability to communicate through the spoken word. The power to use words is a unique and powerful gift.

Our words have the power to destroy and the power to build up. The tongue has the power of life and death. Are we using words to build up people or destroy them? Are they filled with hate or love, bitterness or blessing, complaining or compliments, lust or love, victory or defeat? Like tools they can be used to help us reach our goals or to send us spiraling into a deep depression.

Nelson Mandela, who opposed the South African apartheid regime and was imprisoned for almost 3 decades, knew the power of words. He is often quoted today; but while in prison, his words could not be quoted for fear of repercussion. A decade after his release he said: "It is never my custom to use words lightly. If 27 years in prison have done anything to us, it was to use the silence of solitude to make us understand how precious words are, and how real speech is in its impact on the way people live and die."

Knowing that words are so powerful, you must know that the words you speak is likened to the air you breathe. You must begin to implement your words into words of action. That action will spur change. With our words, we don't have to wait for some other person or some other time; we can speak change now.

You can have a worldwide vision, but can't get out of town because you have small town conversations. Elevate your words. Speak with tremendous purpose and positivity. Talk about your goals and dreams every day.

You can literally (*all pun intended*) change your world by the words you speak. Start talking.

10 years from now make sure you can say you chose your life, you didn't settle for it.

18. What Happened?

By someone I respected, even admired……in the wake of an enormous setback…and what seemed to the world to be an absolute failure; I was being called an imposter, a fraud, a liar, a scoundrel, a fake, irresponsible, etc. I took a verbal beating for something that happened. At that time I had a professional basketball team named the Dallas Generals. The team played in the world famous ABA (American Basketball Association). We were facing some financial difficulties at the time, and my General Manager, Yanika Daniels was letting me have it at the office. She chastised me like never before. Right then, I can't say that I appreciated it. But after those piercing words sunk in, and I embraced them; I thanked her for opening my eyes to the fireball I had become.

As you've heard before….Shit happens!!...and big it did for me.

I didn't let what happened define me. Life is 10% what happens to us, and 90% how we react to it. We are not what happened to us. We are how we respond to what happens to us. I chose not to get bitter, I got better. I didn't let it sink me. I rose to the occasion.

To correct my problems, I first had to acknowledge them. I asked myself, "what happened?" As I took the time to honestly answer myself, I came to a profound conclusion. No longer can I just address the fruit of the problem, I must address the root of the problem. I had so many underlying foundational issues, that everything I built was shaky. I became dedicated, determined, and destined to correct them.

LUCKY BY CHOICE

Difficult and trying times will always introduce themselves to you at the most unexpected times. How you respond and address those introductions will determine how you progress past them.

In life, attitude is everything; it is what shapes our beliefs and our desires. Harsh times will occur throughout our lives, but it is up to us how we interpret them. We are always in control of our emotions despite any given situation.

Many people blame their circumstances for their shortcomings and as a result accept the harsh reality of their situation. These people believe an event is equivalent to its outcome; however, for the truly remarkable person, adversity is where they thrive.

What allows these people to succeed? They realize it is not what has happened to them in their lives, but the manner in which they react to these events. The way a person decides to respond to certain occurrences is what will shape his or her feelings, actions and results. It all lies within ourselves to be successful in life or not.

We can choose to live the life we want, no matter how tough it can get. It is all a matter of mentality, only we will prevent ourselves from achieving greatness. The rest are just small detours before we reach our destinations.

"I am responsible. Although I may not be able to prevent the worst from happening, I am responsible for my attitude toward the inevitable misfortunes that darken life. Bad things do happen; how I respond to them defines my character and the quality of my life. I can choose to sit in perpetual sadness, immobilized by the gravity of my loss, or I can choose to rise from the pain and treasure the most precious gift I have – life itself." ....Walter Anderson

18. What Happened?

Knowledge comes from everything we do and everything that happens to us. We learn valuable lessons over the course of time based on our experiences and the ways in which we react to them. Every hardship presents an opportunity. We just need to recognize that instead of letting it defeat us. Your thoughts and attitude change your experiences and shape your life.

You always have a choice of how you are going to respond to what the world offers you. Do not let something dictate the way you react to things. You need to look within yourself and realize that you have the power to make things happen. We are a sum of all of our life's experiences, so use these past lessons to help better your present situation.

EXCUSES ARE TOOLS OF THE INCOMPETENT. USED TO BUILD MONUMENTS OF NOTHINGNESS. THOSE THAT DWELL WITHIN THEM ARE SELDOM GOOD FOR ANYTHING ELSE.

19. The F Word

Fear is defined as an unpleasant emotion caused by the belief that someone or something is dangerous, likely to cause pain, or a threat. Fear acts in the name of safety. It wants to talk us out of going out on the limb. Why not go out on the limb? That's where all the fruit is!!! It's a form of risk control. Fear is trying to protect you from disappointment and hardship. That is why it's so convincing.

The symptoms of fear are excuses, doubt, and hesitation. Fear grows in the absence of action. International, best-selling author and motivational speaker, Tony Robbins said "When you feel fear, take a step forward."

Fear is the strongest, controlling emotion known to mankind. It is the very thing that we must all overcome in order to move forward with anything in life. It could be about love, family, marriage, school, a job, religion, politics, the economy, finances, a phobia, failure, criticism….or even success. People refuse to take chances, because they fear the criticism which may follow if they fail. The fear of criticism, in such cases is stronger than the desire for success.

Fear causes you to put up a wall, a limit, or mental block in order to protect yourself from the expected danger of moving forward. My friend, Jon Dixon, says that it is very human to form "mental blocks" and "limiting beliefs". We do it all our lives. These are an attempt to interpret the world and survive emotionally. They generally come out of an experience that caused some element of trauma or discomfort or even just a lack of understanding.

Limiting beliefs limit the scope of opportunity that we see in our life. These beliefs are trying to block the chance of disappointment or pain from our accepted reality. It is the minds way of trimming the risks out of our lives. "Stick with what's familiar" it will say. "Don't leave the comfort zone" it will say. Fear is a judgment that we adopt in an emotional situation.

The most common fear is about self worth; the lack of confidence in yourself. How does that manifest? Where does that feeling come from? It comes from "self-talk". That conversation you have with yourself right before any and every decision you have ever made. Your subconscious mind wants to keep you safe in a comfort zone, in familiar territory.

Nothing great ever came from a comfort zone. A mind troubled by fear cannot focus on the course to victory.

So what's the solution you ask? In my opinion, INSPIRATION neutralizes fear.

With inspiration, it will almost always contain some element of risk, or leap of faith, or change of habit. It will take you out of your comfort zone. This means that following your inspiration will not be comfortable. It will ask you to stretch. It will ask you to risk the unknown. It will ask you to venture into unfamiliar territory. If you align with inspiration, it will never fail you if you stay committed. This doesn't mean you will be void of disappointment, that's part of the journey. You will experience trials and errors. These will be the life lessons you need in order to be able to create abundance more effectively.

Many people make the mistake of seeing apparent failures as proof that their fears were right in their warnings. What they

19. The F Word

should believe is that life is trying to teach them the next step. The test you are going through right now contains the opportunity for you to learn the appropriate lesson that you need at this point of your journey. If you truly learn the lesson in that struggle then you won't have to experience that lesson again. Fail to learn the lesson and life will provide another opportunity to learn it. This is why some disappointments seem to repeat in our lives. If you learned what you needed to the first time, you wouldn't need to be taught again.

Learn to recognize the voice of inspiration; that voice from the divinity within you. Make the voice of inspiration part of your decision making process. It is like a muscle, and the more you use and honor it then it will become more recognizable and more obvious to you. It will teach you where to go, and will teach you of your true nature.

Become FEARLESS. Recognize and Declare Your Greatness.

20. More Than Money

Some people know the price of everything, but the value of nothing. I want to briefly share with you my reason for this chapter. Too often, we put all of our focus on the financial benefit of success, and overlook the things that truly hold the value. Through my experience, I've discovered that the things that can't be bought with money hold the most value.

Success is more than money. Reaching a goal that you have set is success. Finding happiness and peace of mind are success. By the way, anything that costs you your peace of mind is too expensive.

Success isn't about how much money you make or wealth you accumulate, it's about the difference you make in people's lives.

There's more to life than money. The truth is, money can't buy everything. For example, money can't buy peace of mind, good friends, a close-knit family, work-life balance, a worry-free day, good karma, time to relax, good health, a golden anniversary, quality time with your kids, a new beginning, natural beauty, happy memories, to name just a few. Many people are actually poor because the only thing they have is money.

I'm not saying that money isn't important. Rather, this is a plea to acknowledge that there's more to life than money. We must assign appropriate value to the intangible areas of our lives, such as our honor, personal relationships, peace of mind, and quality family time, to name a few examples. If we take these things for granted, and lose them as a result, we are on the road to personal bankruptcy.

It's important to keep money in perspective. Do you spend more money satisfying your desires than fulfilling your needs? Do you let money dictate your activities, affect your relationships, and consume your thoughts? Is money a constant cause of anxiety and a source of stress? If you answer yes to these questions, you may be becoming a slave to your money.

I have 8 more questions I want to ask you, and if you answer yes to either one; you are well on your way, if not already, a slave to money.

Let's hope your answer is no to each one.

1. *Are you willing to sacrifice your dreams for more money?*
2. *Are you willing to compromise your honor for more money?*
3. *Are you willing to squander your happiness for more money?*
4. *Are you willing to forgo relationships for more money?*
5. *Are you willing to compromise quality of life for more money?*
6. *Are you willing to forgo peace of mind for more money?*
7. *Are you willing to miss out on life for more money?*
8. *Are you willing to cash in your personal dignity for more money?*

I can only hope that your answer was no to each question. If you answered yes to either one, please reconsider your perspective on life right now. As the old proverb says, "a fool and his money are soon parted."

Do not value money for any more nor any less than it's worth. It is a good servant, but a bad master.

When you look back on your life one day, will you gauge success by the power that you attained and the wealth that you accumulated? Or, will you measure the degree to which your

20. More Than Money

life was rich in character and purpose? Will it matter that you led an honorable existence, made a difference in people's lives, and left the world a better place for your children? Albert Einstein said it well, "Not everything that can be counted counts, and not everything that counts can be counted." The choice is yours. There's more to life than money.

7 RULES OF LIFE

1. Make peace with your past so it does not affect the present.

2. What others think of you is none of your business.

3. Time heals almost everything, give it time.

4. Don't compare your life to others and don't judge them. You have no idea what their journey is all about.

5. It's alright not to know all the answers. They will come to you when you least expect it.

6. You are in charge of your happiness.

7. Smile. You don't own all the problems in the world.

21. It's Not About You

Service is the cornerstone of my foundation. Being considerate to others is my duty. I just want to put it on your heart and tell you that you are not living your life just for you. You have a duty and responsibility to become successful, so that others may benefit from your achievements. It's just about you.

Your outward success will serve as inspiration to someone watching you.

Zig Ziglar said "You can have everything in life you want, if you will just help enough other people get what they want."

Be a servant. More importantly, be a servant-leader. "The servant-leader is servant first... It begins with the natural feeling that one wants to serve, to serve first." - Robert K. Greenleaf. Servant leadership is a philosophy and set of practices that enriches the lives of individuals, builds better organizations and ultimately creates a more just and caring world.

Leadership expert, Skip Prichard states that servant leadership is a blend and balance between leader and servant. You don't lose leadership qualities when becoming a servant leader. Servant leaders lead with others in mind. A servant leader values everyone's contributions and regularly seeks out opinions. Servant leaders cultivate a culture of trust. The replication factor is so important as well. It means teaching others to lead, providing opportunities for growth and demonstrating by example. That means the leader is not always leading, but instead giving up power and deputizing others to lead. The hallmark of a servant leader is encouragement. And a true servant leader says, "Let's go do it," not, "You go do it." A servant leader is the opposite of a dictator. It's a style all about persuading, not commanding. A servant leader is thinking about the next generation, the next leader, the next opportunity. That means a tradeoff between what's important today versus tomorrow, and making choices to benefit the future.

The leader doesn't wear a title as a way to show who's in charge, doesn't think he's better than everyone else, and acts in a way to care for others. In fact, the leader may pick up the trash or clean up a table. Setting an example of service, the servant leader understands that it is not about the leader, but about others.

Servant leaders act with humility; and harmoniously blend characteristics of leadership with service.

In closing, Abraham Lincoln said "The best thing you can do to help a poor person is not be one of them." To me, that statement was about more than money. My interpretation says that you have to be rich in leadership, servitude, and many other intangible qualities in order to help those that are in need, and could be considered poor in many areas of life.

To serve is to love. To serve is to lead.

Everybody can be great, because everybody can serve. You don't have to have a college degree to serve. You don't have to make your subject and your verb agree to serve....You only need a heart full of grace, a soul generated by love.

– Martin Luther King, Jr.

IF - Rudyard Kipling

If you can keep your head when all about you
Are losing theirs and blaming it on you,
If you can trust yourself when all men doubt you,
But make allowance for their doubting too;
If you can wait and not be tired by waiting,
Or being lied about, don't deal in lies,
Or being hated, don't give way to hating,
And yet don't look too good, nor talk too wise:

If you can dream - and not make dreams your master;
If you can think - and not make thoughts your aim;
If you can meet with Triumph and Disaster
And treat those two impostors just the same;
If you can bear to hear the truth you've spoken
Twisted by knaves to make a trap for fools,
Or watch the things you gave your life to, broken,
And stoop and build 'em up with worn-out tools:

If you can make one heap of all your winnings
And risk it on one turn of pitch-and-toss,
And lose, and start again at your beginnings
And never breathe a word about your loss;
If you can force your heart and nerve and sinew
To serve your turn long after they are gone,
And so hold on when there is nothing in you
Except the Will which says to them: 'Hold on!'

If you can talk with crowds and keep your virtue,
Or walk with Kings - nor lose the common touch,
If neither foes nor loving friends can hurt you,
If all men count with you, but none too much;
If you can fill the unforgiving minute
With sixty seconds' worth of distance run,
Yours is the Earth and everything that's in it,
And - which is more - you'll be a Man, my son!

22. Above Reproach

Very briefly, I want to share a story and a bit of advice with you.

One day I was having a heart to heart conversation with my frat brother, Kira Lane. ….he called it a "come to Jesus" meeting with him. He wanted to let me know that although I am doing well in life, there are some things in my past that may come back to haunt me. Out of the whole conversation, the thing that stuck to me the most was when he said "from this point forward, stay about reproach."

I took a moment to analyze our conversation. What I gathered from it was this…..my past is what it is, and I can't change it. But what I can do is control my present and future. I should act and carry on day by day in a manner that protects me from unwarranted criticism. I should strive to be blameless.

As we parted ways, I let him know that in 2009, I began to challenge myself to live by and on a five star platform in which the attributes of Dedication, Discipline, Excellence, Integrity, and Respect lead the way. I adopted those attributes in an attempt to steady my life's course; develop my character; strengthen my integrity; protect and restore my reputation; and most of all, hold myself accountable with my goals and dreams.

My advice and encouragement to you is to live a life that is free from reproach. As you go through your journey, you will need to avoid as much damage as possible. Be careful with your thoughts, words, and actions.

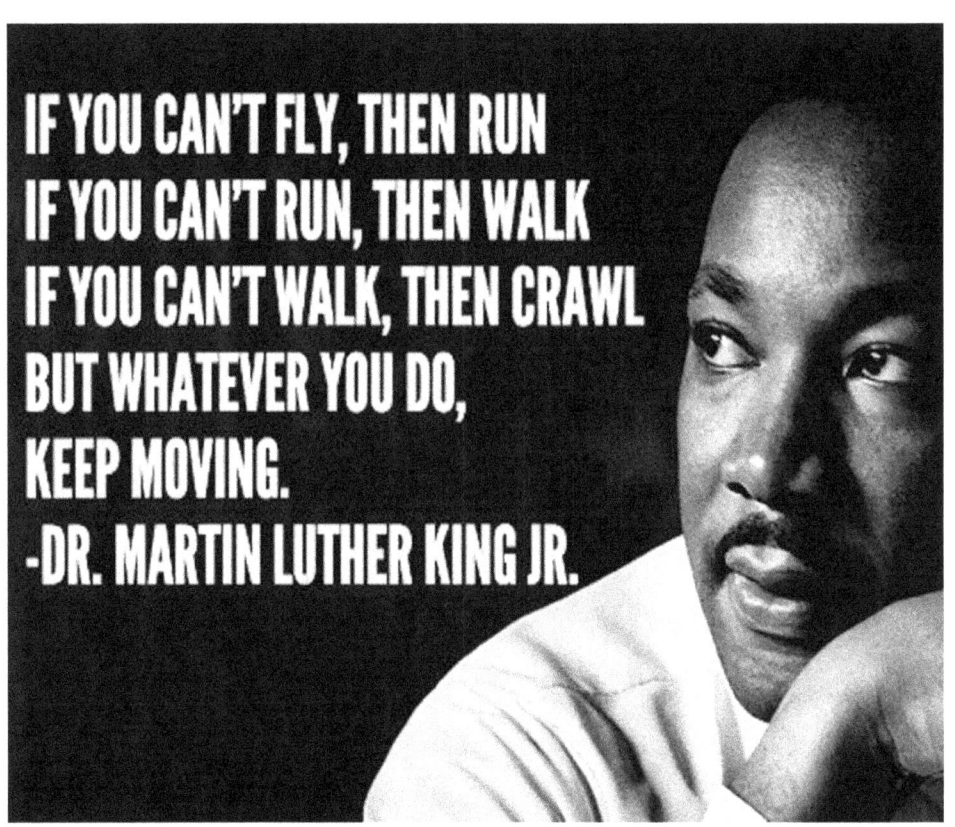

23. Consequences & Repercussions

My favorite movie of all time is LIFE, with Eddie Murphy and Martin Lawrence. It came out in 1999. There was a scene in the movie when they were eating, and a character by the name of Goldmouth asked Claude Banks (Martin Lawrence)…" You gon' eat yo' cornbread!" Claude didn't understand the consequences attached to giving up his cornbread to Goldmouth while in prison, but Ray Gibson (Eddie Murphy) did. So Ray tells Goldmouth no, and that Claude is going to eat his own cornbread. Then it shifts….Goldmouth says to Ray, " maybe I ought to eat yo' cornbread"….and Rays response was "….it's gon' be consequences and repercussions." If you've seen the movie, you know the rest….and hopefully I got a chuckle out of you. If you haven't seen the movie, shame on you. So yes, once again; a movie has inspired a chapter in the book.

I've shared some very personal and private stories about my life with you. Ironically, when that movie came out, I was in federal prison watching it. Maybe that's why it has such an impact on me. In chapter 16, I gave you some insight about when I was on the run from the police. I, Keio Gamble, was a fugitive for seven years!! On the day I made the choice not to be caught, I changed the direction of my life. Eventually I came to the conclusion that I'd been on that road too long, and needed to find my way back home. I made some bad decisions, and needed to face the consequences and repercussions. I needed some help. My plea for help could only be answered by me. I was the problem, and the solution.

Being on the run taught me an increased level of discretion, patience, understanding and forgiveness. My freedom meant so much to me that, because of the repercussions, I started to think with self-preservation in mind. There are many actions in which as a people we decide to take, knowing the consequences will not be as severe. Once I decided to keep in mind the severe consequences, my decision making became a lot better. There were small things that I did different, such as how I dressed, where I went, and most of all…who I spent my time with.

A lot of times, right before we make decisions, we analyze the consequence of our next action. If some kind of way, we can justify our action, whether right or wrong, it's because we don't fear the repercussion.

Now, I know it seems strange, but imagine this……….going to jail wasn't all that bad for me. Why would I say that you ask?!?!?! It forced me to regroup myself. I had plenty of time to think about what I did to land me where I was. It afforded me the opportunity to reorganize and fine tune my thinking process.

When making decisions that are pivotal, or may be a detriment; the idea is to minimize the negative consequences that compound the trials of life without the additional burden of the consequences of poor choices.

To sum it up, you must know and accept that there will be consequences and repercussions for every decision you make; good or bad. Your decision may not only affect you. Be mindful of the outcome of the choices you make.

Choices
Chances
Changes
You must make a <u>choice</u> to take a <u>chance</u> or your life will never <u>change</u>.

24. Black & White

Short, sweet, simple, and to the point; as black and white matters tend to be.

Do you see the world and the decisions you make as black and white or in shades of gray?

People who see the world as "black and white" tend to speak their mind more or make quick decisions; be more predictable in making decisions; and be less anxious about making wrong choices.

People who see the world in "shades of gray" tend to procrastinate or avoid making decisions if possible; feel more regret after making decisions; and appreciate multiple points of view.

For the sake of reaching your personal goals, I lean more towards black and white, and stay away from gray areas. The black and white usually signifies more definiteness and decisiveness; while the gray area personifies uncertainty.

To accomplish goals as big as you need to possess, there has to be an uncontested amount of certainty that anchors your vision. To you I say, "draw a line in the stand!!" Claim your destiny. Make it as clear and simple as black and white. Have enough courage and conviction to stand by your decision.

Let's talk leadership for a moment.

Leadership begins and ends with trust. Trust is built on a foundation of the constancy of your character. You cannot effectively serve those you lead if you fail to earn and keep their trust. Black and white thinkers are sometimes labeled as possessing a clear view of right and wrong. People who display the clarity and confidence to consistently do the right thing regardless of the current situation have reached a level of leadership maturity to be applauded.

So to you I say this….whether you are working on yourself alone, or you are a dynamic leader that shepherds a team that believes in you. As clear as the distinction is between black and white, you must remain definite in action, decisive, transparent and inclusive, and courageous. As easy as it can be to just blend in with the crowd in the gray area, resist it. You and those who follow you will appreciate it later, if not now.

The Cambridge Dictionary says that a black-and-white subject or situation is one in which it is easy to understand what is right and wrong. Why complicate life? Keep the majority of your dealings black and white.

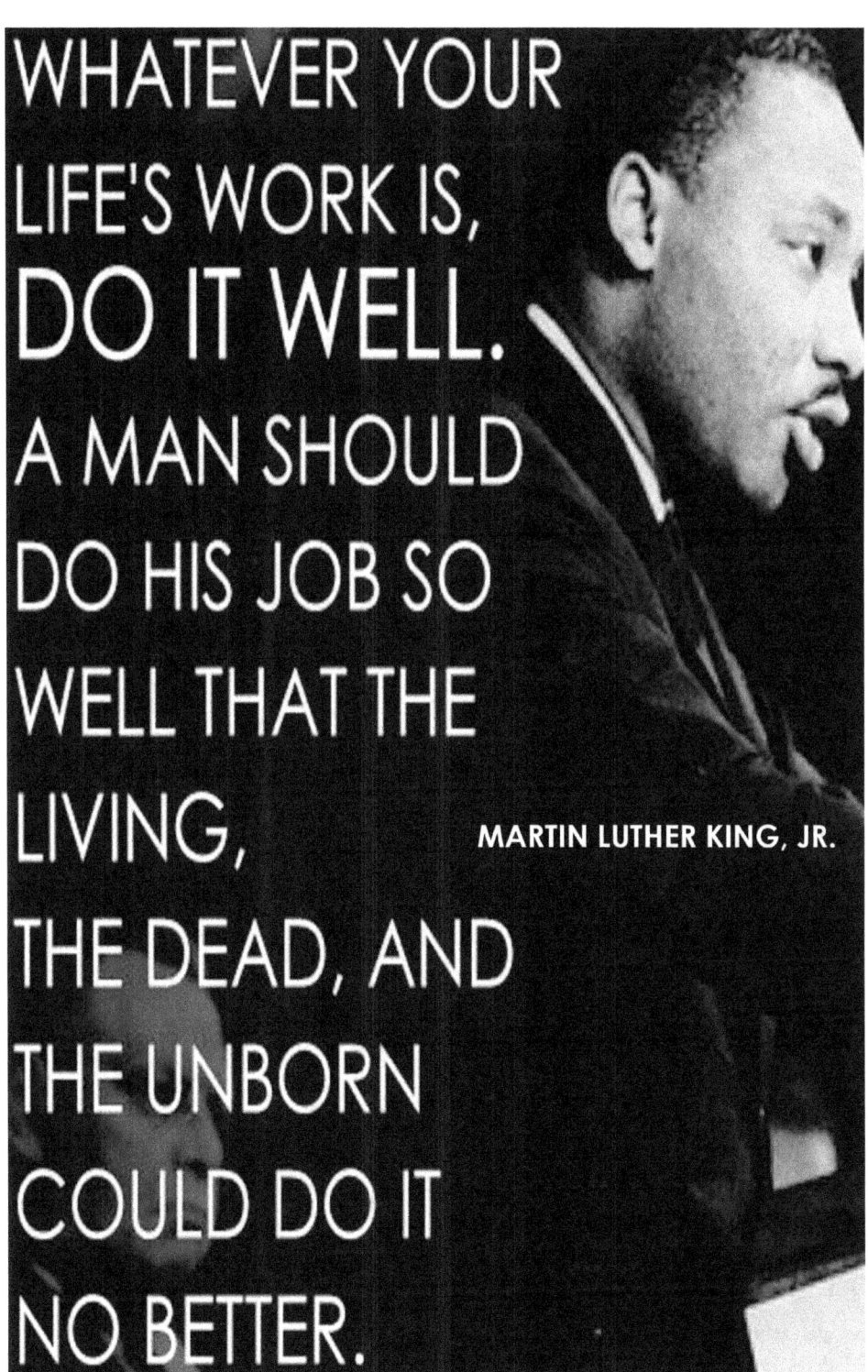

25. Does Size Matter?

*If your dreams don't scare you or make you uncomfortable,
they are not big enough.*

The one major factor that separates the most successful people from the rest begins with a single thought. This single thought — if cultivated — grows over time into the empowering habit of thinking big that eventually takes over a person's psychology, and propels them towards the achievement of their goals and objectives.

We must, however, keep in mind that over years this single thought is analyzed, criticized and condemned by others. People believe that this thought is impossible, improbably and undeniably unimaginable. They say that the thought is unorthodox and bordering on crazy. And so this single thought must overcome great obstacles, setbacks, problems and difficulties before it can realize its full potential. After all, this single thought understands that in order to grow BIG and expand, that it must accept the harsh realities of life and respond by growing long and strong roots that will support its tremendous weight as it stretches towards the sky. Yes, this single thought knows very well indeed that to think big, is to do big.

You must think big without any reservations and without any hesitation in order to contribute more, learn more, become more and stretch yourself and your own abilities beyond their current psychological limitations.

The key to shifting your perspective and developing the habit of thinking big involves stepping outside of yourself and into another persona — essentially becoming someone you are not, yet someone who will help you see things a little BIGGER, better and far more creatively.

In order to think big you must think from the perspective of having no limitations and no fears. It's as though life is conspiring in your favor, breaking down all walls and obstacles that are standing in your way, thus releasing your unlimited potential to develop the habit of thinking big, acting big, and doing bigger things than you ever thought were possible.

Thinking big is not easy. It's something that we must learn to cultivate over time on a daily basis in everything we do. However, even when this habit of thinking big is deeply ingrained into our psyche, there will still be times when barriers will need to be overcome, obstacles will need to be surpassed, and old habits will need to be broken. It is during these times that we need to think big and do bigger things than ever before.

I dare you to think bigger, to act bigger, and to be bigger, and I promise you a richer and more exciting life if you do.

So to answer the question, yes…….size does matter.

26. Conversation Ruled The Nation, But Understanding Conquered The World

The most difficult phase of life is not when no one understands you. It's when you don't understand yourself.

I believe it is very paramount to be able to communicate verbally, at a higher level than most, in order to reach your goals and succeed in life. Being able to articulate your thoughts, wishes, desires, and goals is the precursor to the understanding you need the world to have of you.

Personally, I love to use analogies and comparisons when speaking. My goal is to get the listener to see what I'm saying. I really want them to be able to visualize my words as I paint a picture with each noun, verb, adverb, and adjective serving the purpose as a verbal paintbrush.

Seek first to understand, then to be understood. Often, I've frustrated people because I won't drop or walk away from a conversation, debate, sometimes an argument. Why? Because I want to make sure that no matter what, there is an understanding. Whether we agree with each other or not, let's understand why. I would say, "help me understand."

It was around 1999/2000 that I really got into politics; more so political campaigns. The thing that I noticed was that the person that won any election was the one that spoke the best, and the people felt they understood. More specifically, let's talk Presidents of the United States. The conversation they had during the campaign by way of speeches and debates was what won them the nation. The ultimate respect for a President comes when the rest of the world understands him. Think about it……How did the majority of the world receive Barack Obama vs Donald Trump?; Bill Clinton vs George Bush?; John F. Kennedy vs Richard Nixon? "See what I'm saying." Their conversation won them the nation. Their understanding won them the world, or not. All before any work or implementation is done to prove their true ability.

Again, the power of words is an awesome, magnificent gift that we all possess.

I've been notorious for driving my position on conversation taking talking and listening. Sarcastically, especially when the conversation is intense, I would say, "conversation takes talking and listening….when I talk, you listen." Okay, okay….kind of harsh I know. But it's one hell of an attention getter. Likewise, when someone else is talking…I'm definitely listening. I'm intensely listening so that I can understand their conversation and try to "see what they are saying."

Most people only listen to respond, so the opportunity to fully understand the other person is missed because they are already preparing their response and stance. Take the time and really listen to other people. Not just hear them, but truly listen. People will tell you everything you need to know if you'd just listen long enough.

I've grown and developed as a great conversationalist, but an even better listener. I challenge you to listen more than you talk. You know the natural math. You have one mouth, and two ears; act accordingly.

Lastly, in an effort to reach your goals and dreams; please seek to get an understanding of the who, what, where, when,

26. Conversation Ruled The Nation, But Understanding Conquered The World

why, and how you do everything in life. Once you understand that, you will be able to clearly articulate your conversation on your purpose, reasons, goals, and dreams to the point where the majority will understand you with ease; and you will be well on your way on your unique road to success.

Part Three:

THE WINNERS' CIRCLE

27. Wax On, Wax Off

As Benjamin Franklin said, "Tell me and I forget, teach me and I may remember, involve me and I learn." When I was starting out, I had no idea what was involved in running a business, including making a business plan, budgeting, handling daily operations, making strategic decisions or running a marketing campaign. Hell, I was a Biology major with no business background at all. I didn't have a mentor there from the start. I didn't tap into a wealth of knowledge to get me up to speed faster and shorten my learning curve. I took loss after loss. In life, just as in business, we need mentors.

In 1984, there was a movie called "The Karate Kid." In the movie, there were two main characters; Daniel and Mr. Miyagi. In the beginning of the film, "the new kid in school" Daniel spends his time getting pummeled by a gang of pretty boy thugs. Then one night during a routine beating, a seemingly old, frail Japanese man, "Mr. Miyagi" comes out of nowhere, completely manhandles the thugs, and saves Daniel. Daniel is astonished at Mr. Miyagi's ability to beat up a bunch of well-trained karate buffs without breaking a sweat, so he begs Mr. Miyagi to train him so he can defend himself from further punishment.

His first lesson is cleaning and waxing his master's car. His master tells him to "Wax On, Wax Off."

Miyagi becomes Daniel's teacher and, slowly, a surrogate father figure. He begins Daniel's training by having him perform laborious chores such as waxing cars, sanding a wooden floor, refinishing a fence, and painting Miyagi's house.

Each chore is accompanied with a specific movement, such as clockwise/counter-clockwise hand motions.

Daniel fails to see any connection to his training from these hard chores and eventually feels frustrated, believing he has learned nothing of karate. When he expresses his frustration, Miyagi reveals that Daniel has been learning defensive blocks through muscle memory learned by performing the chores.

Mr. Miyagi shows him all of the specific tasks he had been doing and how they transferred into karate. At the end of the transfer of learning phase of his training Daniel is amazed at what he had "learned"; when he thought he was just doing everyday tasks.

In the final scene, Daniel goes on to face the toughest, most skilled karate student in the All-Valley Karate Tournament championship, and WINS!!!

There are some skills you can learn on your own, and some you can try to learn, but if you intend to take the journey of mastery, the best thing you can do is to arrange for first-rate instruction. For mastering most skills, there's nothing better than being in the hands of a mentor, either one-on-one or in a small group.

We can only self-teach so much! A solid mentor can provide us with information we need to send us on the right track faster. It might be a mentor, a coach, paid or unpaid, or someone we look up to who has the experience and passion to help us improve. You don't have to know that person personally, although it helps. Most of my mentors I claim through studying and reading about what they have done to be successful. I've never met them in person, or even had a conversation with them; but I learn from them.

27. Wax On, Wax Off

I've had several mentors over the years and learned a large amount of valuable life lessons from each and every one of them. From what personal decisions to make, to not making certain business decisions, to fostering certain partnerships, a mentor can help guide you through your life or entrepreneurial journey.

Inspirational entrepreneur, Oprah Winfrey stated, "A mentor is someone who allows you to see the hope inside yourself." They are there no matter what and offer moral support sprinkled heavily with cheerleading. Mentors can see where we need to improve where we often cannot. The delicate balance of mentoring someone is not creating them in your own image, but giving them the opportunity to create themselves. They are disciplinarians that create necessary boundaries that we cannot set for ourselves; sounding boards so we can bounce ideas off them for an unfiltered opinion; most importantly, mentors have the experiences you can learn from to prevent making the same mistakes beginners make.

Having a mentor is not a sign of weakness; it shows you are smart enough and are driven enough to succeed.

28. Play To Win

This just may be the shortest chapter you will ever read in life. I don't feel that a lot has to be said to convey the message of this chapter. PLAY TO WIN is a mindset that consistent winners possess. Your mindset determines your success.

Winners think a certain way, and losers think a certain way. Winners don't wait for chances, they take them. Winners don't just compete, they dominate. Winners make more moves, and less announcements.

Einstein said, "you have to learn the rules of the game, and then you have to play better than anyone else." Learn the rules of the game of winning!

Some people try to play it safe, or play not to lose. Why play at all, if you are not playing to win?!?!?!?!

The message in this chapter is short, sweet, simple, and to the point. Give yourself permission to live a big life. Step into who you are meant to be. Stop playing small. You are meant for greater things. PLAY TO WIN!!!

THE LION & THE GAZELLE

EVERY MORNING IN AFRICA, A GAZELLE WAKES UP.

IT KNOWS IT MUST RUN FASTER THAN THE FASTEST LION

OR IT WILL BE KILLED.

EVERY MORNING IN AFRICA, A LION WAKES UP.

IT KNOWS IT MUST OUTRUN THE SLOWEST GAZELLE

OR IT WILL STARVE TO DEATH.

IT DOESN'T MATTER WHETHER YOU ARE A LION OR A GAZELLE;

WHEN THE SUN COMES UP, YOU'D BETTER BE RUNNING.

African Proverb

29. Tune In To Your Star Player

Poor Little Tink Tink……Do you remember that hilarious stand-up comedy show when Katt Williams told us his version of Oscar Pistorius? I laugh until tears flow down my face every time I see it, but I received the message and inspiration from Katt; so much so, that I named the chapter from what he said, when he said "You gon' have to be in tune with your star fucking player cuz these haters do not play fair….."

In 2007, Oscar Pistorious participated in his first international competition for able-bodied athletes, and after the race he was disqualified under claims that he had "an unfair advantage." Due to this controversy, Pistorius was required to undergo a series of scientific tests, which ultimately affirmed that his prosthetic limbs use 25% less energy and 30% less lifting of the body than those able-bodied runners. In the eyes of scientific terms, this indeed does prove that Pistorius carries an advantage over able-bodied runners. However, Pistorius did not let this affirmation hold him back and he continued on fighting for his dream in participating in the 2008 Olympics.

As Katt Williams tells the story of Pistorius being disqualified from a race he had already participated in. He dubs Pistorius the nickname "Tink Tink"; undoubtedly due to the supposed noise he makes as he runs. With his hilariously sarcastic, high-pitched voice and his noticeably small 5'5" frame, he says not only did Tink Tink start running, but he started winning…." And the last place you want to be, in a motherfucking foot race, is behind the motherfucker with no god damn foots!" …and then he continues to say "these hating ass motherfuckers at the Olympic committee let this motherfucker race, and then waited until he won, and then disqualified him and said, and I quote, he had "an unfair advantage."" He then looks at the audience with the most perplexed look on his face, pauses, raises his hand, and proceeds to say, "are you talking about the motherfucker running with no god damn legs? Is that who the fuck you talking 'bout?" The audience bursts into laughter. It is the irony of the situation that makes his joke so comical, a man with no legs being deemed as having an unfair advantage. Most people in life would view his circumstance as just the opposite. Katt Williams describes "Poor Little Tink Tink's" racing legs as "bent back paper clips... like two baby boomerangs." The audience is almost silent after this comment is made, unsure of whether to laugh or not. Katt Williams then chimes in with "Don't try to act like something wrong with me, some of you motherfuckers saw the story you know what the fuck I'm talking about, it look like bent back paper clips!" And once again, like all of his jokes, laughter takes over the arena in Washington, DC.

Katt Williams' story of "Poor Little Tink Tink" ultimately has a happy ending. After the Olympic Committee stated he could not participate, Oscar Pistorius took his determination to another level and appealed their ruling. After a two-day hearing, the Court of Arbitration for Sport revoked the committee's decision with immediate effect. Oscar Pistorius went on to claim three Gold medals in the 2008 Olympics, and two Gold medals and one Silver medal in the 2012 Olympics.

I know some of you may have just finished reading that and thought, my goodness!! Did he just really write that?? And my answer is…..Why yes I did!!

Sometimes, you have to tell the story just the way it is. In that story, like many others; the message is about overcoming adversity by focusing, being passionate, and having an

29. Tune In To Your Star Player

uncontested level of commitment to yourself and your goals. You can't allow yourself to be distracted by naysayers and negative influences. The quickest way to be defeated is to be distracted.

You have to remain focused and tuned in to your vision, desires, goals, dreams, wants, and needs in life. Einstein was no genius. He was just tuned in to his star player. He was considered a genius because of his tremendous focus.

Just like the antenna on a radio, TV, or cell phone has to be tuned in to get the right frequency and clear signal, you do too.

There will be people that want to see you do good, but not better than them. So you have to know that favor ain't fair, and be ready to tune in to what lies deep beneath your skin in order to achieve greatness.

The same boiling water that softens potatoes hardens eggs. It's all about what you are made of, not your circumstances. You have to dig deep down inside to find your star player. It's there. There is nothing outside of yourself that can ever enable you to get better, richer, stronger, or smarter. Everything is within. Everything exists. Seek nothing outside of yourself.

Before I close this chapter, I want to share a story with you. It's a powerful story about the greatness hidden in each of us that we will find if we would just tune in to our star player.

Over three hundred years ago, the Burmese army planned an attack to invade Thailand. At the time, the country was known as Siam. The Siamese monks were in possession of the most amazing Buddha statue. The statue is over 10 feet tall and weighs in excess of 2 1/2 tons. It is made of solid gold and is valued today at over $200 MILLION dollars. The monks were determined to protect the shrine that meant so much to them. While it was priceless to them for reasons that transcend money; they knew that the Burmese would stop at nothing to steal the statue because of its tremendous monetary value. They covered the Golden Buddha with 12 inches of clay knowing that the warriors would totally ignore it and think it worthless. Sadly, the monks were slaughtered in the invasion and the secret of the Golden Buddha stayed hidden for two centuries. The Buddha itself though, remained safe.

In the mid 50's, a monastery was to be relocated to make room for a new highway. The monks arranged for a crane to come and move the "Clay" Buddha to its new location. When the crane started to lift the statue, it was much heavier than expected and it began to crack. Wanting to protect the priceless shrine, the monks lowered it back down and decided to wait until the next day to bring more powerful equipment. To add insult to injury, the rains came so the monks lovingly covered the statue with tarps to keep the moisture away. In the dark of night, the head monk took his flashlight and went out to make sure the Buddha was adequately covered. When the light of the flashlight shined into the crack of the clay, he saw a glimmer...a reflection of something underneath that shroud of clay. He immediately started to carefully chisel away shards of clay to find that the glimmer grew brighter. Hours later, and all the clay removed...he was in the presence of a Buddha made of solid gold. It now resides in The Temple of the Golden Buddha in Bangkok, Thailand. Every year, millions of people go there to see this magnificent work of art and to worship at his feet. And to think, it may never have been uncovered...

I love this story for so many reasons; but, I think it is such a representation of what we do to ourselves as we develop in life. We come into this world as little miracles. We are creative and

29. Tune In To Your Star Player

true to ourselves. We believe in luck, magic, and dreams. In an effort to protect ourselves, we start layering on all these protective coatings. We subscribe to fear where there is none. We subscribe to doubt where there shouldn't be because we don't ever want to be disappointed. In the long run these things turn into self imposed limitations in our subconscious minds. They become part of an auto-pilot system that can steer us away from our true destiny. They block us from achieving our full potential. Mostly, the recognition that they are even there can go unnoticed for years. Think about it... the gold underneath that Buddha stayed hidden for centuries!!!!

There is a Golden Buddha underneath your skin.

You have to get focused and dedicated to the excellence within yourselves. **TUNE IN TO YOUR STAR PLAYER.**

30. Difficult Takes A Day, Impossible Takes A Week

*"Impossible is just a big word thrown around
by small men who find it easier to live in
the world they've been given,
than to explore the power they have to change it.
Impossible is not a fact. It's an opinion.
Impossible is not a declaration. It's a dare.
Impossible is potential.
Impossible is temporary.
Impossible is nothing."*

~Muhammad Ali~

Overcoming the impossible is a challenge laid before every person in one way or another. Most of the time, when facing a situation or circumstance that we've never faced before, we feel intimidated and a bit hesitant. Conquering what seems to be impossible begins with a winner's mindset. Winners take complicated things and make them simple. Losers take simple things and complicate them.

Rarely, does a dream or goal come true easily and effortlessly, without delays, problems or hurdles. It is far more common, however, that you have to overcome many obstacles and suffer some pain before achieving any meaningful target. The bigger your dreams, the tougher your challenge; the more ambitious your goals, the more likely it is that you will face difficulties on your way towards them.

When this happens, what will you do? Will you just give up? Or will you persist and struggle and succeed?

A lot of that depends upon your attitude and experience. Some of it depends upon your skills and network. The majority depends on your thinking. As Henry Ford stated, "whether you think you can or whether you think you can't, you're right."

Achieving the perceived impossible all starts with positive thinking. You've heard the old saying, "where there's a will, there's a way." Being willing to tackle the challenge is half the battle. You must be able to look at difficulty and say, "small thing to a giant, I can overcome this."

Life will present some challenges that seem so impossible and difficult that it feels like digging in concrete with a plastic spoon.

Too often, we tend to focus on the problems and difficulties along our journey. Stop. Look for solutions. Our mind tends to find whatever we are looking for. If we're seeking out excuses to fail or to justify our decision not to push forward, we'll find them – in the form of setbacks, constraints and limitations. But if we obsess about finding a way past any of these restraints and breaking through to the level of success we set out in search of, then we discover these solutions. Impossible is only the figment of an insufficient imagination.

During one of the worst periods of my life (because of my bad decisions), I was beset by problems from many different directions. Each one had the potential to destroy me and all I had worked hard to build over the years. All of them happened simultaneously! By choosing to focus on solutions instead of reveling in my troubles, I found them. One by one, I began conquering the impossible. I'm not saying that it wasn't difficult. I'm just saying it wasn't impossible.

30. Difficult Takes A Day, Impossible Takes A Week

Simply said, difficult is what takes a little time; the impossible is what takes a little longer.

Impossible is just a starting point.

There's a poem titled *See It Through* by Edgar A. Guest. I'm reminded of an excerpt from it every time I face a seemingly impossible situation. I'm going to share only the excerpt with you, and want you to really key in and focus on the meaning of these few words.

> *"Even hope may seem but futile,*
> *When with troubles you're beset,*
> *But remember you are facing*
> *Just what other men have met."*

To me it says when it seems all hope is gone, and you have encountered the impossible, and the troubles are overwhelming; think about the fact that some other person has faced this same "impossible" problem, and overcame it. So why can't you?

You will be on a forever journey of many miles that won't be an easy walk. You will have hardships to endure, mountains to climb, and deep water to tread. That journey is your life. The vehicle is you. The navigator is your mindset.

Choosing your path in life will definitely come with perceived impossibilities and degrees of difficulty.

Don't miss out on something that could be truly amazing, just because it could also be difficult. Impossible only means that you haven't found the solution yet.

IT COULDN'T BE DONE
EDGAR A. GUEST

SOMEBODY SAID THAT IT COULDN'T BE DONE
BUT HE WITH A CHUCKLE REPLIED
THAT "MAYBE IT COULDN'T," BUT HE WOULD BE ONE
WHO WOULDN'T SAY SO TILL HE'D TRIED.
SO HE BUCKLED RIGHT IN WITH THE TRACE OF A GRIN
ON HIS FACE. IF HE WORRIED HE HID IT.
HE STARTED TO SING AS HE TACKLED THE THING
THAT COULDN'T BE DONE, AND HE DID IT!

SOMEBODY SCOFFED: "OH, YOU'LL NEVER DO THAT;
AT LEAST NO ONE EVER HAS DONE IT;"
BUT HE TOOK OFF HIS COAT AND HE TOOK OFF HIS HAT
AND THE FIRST THING WE KNEW HE'D BEGUN IT.
WITH A LIFT OF HIS CHIN AND A BIT OF A GRIN,
WITHOUT ANY DOUBTING OR QUIDDIT,
HE STARTED TO SING AS HE TACKLED THE THING
THAT COULDN'T BE DONE, AND HE DID IT.

THERE ARE THOUSANDS TO TELL YOU IT CANNOT BE DONE,
THERE ARE THOUSANDS TO PROPHESY FAILURE,
THERE ARE THOUSANDS TO POINT OUT TO YOU ONE BY ONE,
THE DANGERS THAT WAIT TO ASSAIL YOU.
BUT JUST BUCKLE IN WITH A BIT OF A GRIN,
JUST TAKE OFF YOUR COAT AND GO TO IT;
JUST START IN TO SING AS YOU TACKLE THE THING
THAT "CANNOT BE DONE," AND YOU'LL DO IT.

31. The Harder I Work, The Luckier I Get

Thomas Jefferson said, "I'm a great believer in luck, and I find the harder I work the more I have of it."

This chapter is about the relationship between work and luck. Often actors, entrepreneurs, and other people long to get that one "lucky break," forgetting perhaps the combination of opportunity, preparation, and hard work that most success takes.

I used to have a riddle that I would ask people….."Do you know how many years it takes to become an overnight success? Funny right? If it takes more than overnight, then it's not an overnight success. Never mind the fact that I asked how many years.

The truth of the matter is that there are few true overnight successes. Behind what looks like sudden success, is often years of hard work, trial and error, and failures. But the harder you work, the more good ideas and chances you may make for yourself.

It's not about how bad you want it. It's about how hard you are willing to work for it. You can't hope for it more than you work for it.

So many people out there seem to believe that successful people just got lucky; that they somehow just woke up one day and were rich or famous or respected. Some were, no doubt, but the vast majority of successful people are successful because of very specific, deliberate actions that they took.

LUCKY BY CHOICE

I was once told by a really cool guy I met in a real estate seminar, Bob Thornton, that LUCK stands for Laboring Under Correct Knowledge. He pointed out some information that said a great strategy is key to getting lucky in business. The more systematic and scalable your approach is, the luckier you will get. The same goes for life.

The beauty of hard work is that it typically pays off, even if not in the measure that was anticipated.

Opportunity is missed by most people because it is dressed in overalls and looks like hard work. Every entrepreneur will tell you that their life didn't revolve around an easy journey up to the top. Instead, it was a maze of obstacles and barricades that they had to learn to navigate around. They will also tell you that despite working smart, there is still no substitute for working hard. Nothing can replace your effort, and your so-called " luck" depends on your effort first.

Luck doesn't have much to do with success. You and you alone determine your faith and success by hard work, positioning, leveraging, and driving yourself to succeed.

> "WHEN YOU WANT TO SUCCEED AS BAD AS YOU WANT TO BREATHE, THEN YOU'LL BE SUCCESSFUL."
>
> Eric Thomas

32. Keep Yourself In Fighting Trim

Black may be the clouds about you
and your future may seem grim,
But don't let your nerve desert you;
Keep yourself in fighting trim.

Those words became very significant to me in the Spring of 1996. They come from a poem that I referenced earlier in the book, See It Through. The process of pledging was intense, to say the least. It required that I was in physical, mental, and emotional shape. Every fiber of my being was challenged during that time. It provided the groundwork for me to be able to claim an advantage in life. I was being trained to persevere, overcome, and uplift.

In order to prepare yourself to conquer life, you must have the correct fitness; be in fighting trim. Physical, mental, emotional, spiritual, and financial fitness will be required to conquer all that life will throw your way. The key is to always attain and apply the knowledge to grow and strengthen those needed components.

I like to look at life like a war with many battles that must be fought. Each of the 5 components listed above are of absolute importance to your success in life; personally and professionally. There are definite battlefronts that you must dominate.

A person who is fit is capable of living life to its fullest extent.

Physical and mental fitness play very important roles in your lives and people who are both, physically and mentally fit are less prone to medical conditions. If a person is physically fit, but mentally unwell or troubled, he or she will not be able to function optimally. Mental fitness can only be achieved if your body is functioning well. You can help relax your own mind and eliminate stresses by exercising regularly and eating right. In order to maintain a relaxed state of mind, a person should be physically active. A person who is fit both physically and mentally is strong enough to face the ups and downs of life, and is not affected by drastic changes if they take place.

Emotional fitness is an essential trait. A quality that is more important than physical capabilities. In professional sports, the difference physically between one athlete and another is actually pretty minuscule. To be at that level, all professional athletes must be incredibly physically fit. While one may be a bit faster than another in a race toward the end zone, or stronger than another when they want to wrestle the ball away, what really differentiates super athletes who win championships from the rest of the crowd is emotional fitness. Being stable and self-aware, especially in the face of adversity, creates a positive mindset that allows you to create opportunity. These qualities avoid a situation where a hardship can get into your head and dictate your decision making. Those who lack emotional fitness are more apt to become frustrated, angry, and irrational; which will all lead to poor decision making. Our emotional fitness is exemplified by the way we conduct ourselves when facing adversity.

Spiritual fitness is a process, a pursuit. One thing I can tell you about spiritual fitness is this–from personal experience I know that when my soul gets "fitter" I experience more peace, less stress. When I am growing in spiritual fitness I feel stronger mentally and emotionally so I can face the challenges of the day—whether it is active little ones or something much harder than that. And just like physical fitness, spiritual fitness

32. Keep Yourself In Fighting Trim

is a daily, ongoing process. We get weaker spiritually when we don't focus on it. This is a fact about spiritual fitness. Spirituality can mean something different to everyone. It is often defined by a person's beliefs, upbringing, and life experiences. Spirituality may be used generally to refer to that which gives meaning and purpose in life, or the term may be used specifically to refer to the practice of a philosophy, religion, or way of living. Whatever it means to you, be sure to nurture, protect, and develop your spirit. It is your source of energy and sanity.

Last, but not least; financial fitness is the state of the financial system associated with our personal lives. It is that marvelously complex system that compiles our physical materialistic behaviors into a numerical financial representation. In other words, our financial fitness is all about making informed financial decisions in our day to day life.

Since such system touches on every single aspect of our daily lives, now and forever that we are alive, be it materialistic or sentimental, the bottle of water we buy or that shopping spree that we enjoy, they are all in the system…. our personal financial system. It is a must that we keep a close eye on it and make sure that it is healthy and fit. Obtaining and maintaining financial fitness is as important as obtaining and maintaining physical fitness. Both need to be programmed into our daily life cycle and be an essential part of it.

Knowing that our financial health is important, we should strive to keep it fit. Keeping it fit takes time, effort, patience, discipline, and determination. Again just like our physical fitness, we need to work it out over periods of time, put some effort into it, be patience on the results, have a high level of discipline and determination to see the results. The lack of financial fitness will definitely cause problems that will compromise all of the other fitness components. It's been said that "money isn't everything, but having it is." There is almost nothing in life that doesn't require money or finances to obtain it.

The financial position you are in today will not be the financial position you are in tomorrow — it will either be better or worse. Change is inevitable. You cannot stop change from taking place; you can only determine the direction it will take. You know better than anyone else the rewards associated with the way you currently interact with your finances. Achieving long-term financial fitness takes courage, discipline, sacrifice, and consistent effort, but the rewards can be extraordinary. What direction will you choose?

In closing, you have to be prepared for the sprints and marathons of your day-to-day and long term livelihood. Physical, mental, emotional, spiritual, and financial fitness will be the cornerstones of your success. Give yourself ample time to develop and maintain each component, so that when the clouds about you may seem dimmed, and your future may seem grim; you won't let your nerve desert you, because you will be in fighting trim.

SEE IT THROUGH
BY EDGAR ALBERT GUEST

WHEN YOU'RE UP AGAINST A TROUBLE,
MEET IT SQUARELY, FACE TO FACE;
LIFT YOUR CHIN AND SET YOUR SHOULDERS,
PLANT YOUR FEET AND TAKE A BRACE.
WHEN IT'S VAIN TO TRY TO DODGE IT,
DO THE BEST THAT YOU CAN DO;
YOU MAY FAIL, BUT YOU MAY CONQUER,
SEE IT THROUGH!

BLACK MAY BE THE CLOUDS ABOUT YOU
AND YOUR FUTURE MAY SEEM GRIM,
BUT DON'T LET YOUR NERVE DESERT YOU;
KEEP YOURSELF IN FIGHTING TRIM.
IF THE WORST IS BOUND TO HAPPEN,
SPITE OF ALL THAT YOU CAN DO,
RUNNING FROM IT WILL NOT SAVE YOU,
SEE IT THROUGH!

EVEN HOPE MAY SEEM BUT FUTILE,
WHEN WITH TROUBLES YOU'RE BESET,
BUT REMEMBER YOU ARE FACING
JUST WHAT OTHER MEN HAVE MET.
YOU MAY FAIL, BUT FALL STILL FIGHTING;
DON'T GIVE UP, WHATE'ER YOU DO;
EYES FRONT, HEAD HIGH TO THE FINISH.
SEE IT THROUGH!

33. You Miss 100% Of The Shots You Don't Take

*Successful people make decisions quickly
and rarely ever change their mind.
Unsuccessful people make decisions slowly,
or never, and often change their mind.*

Choices are like free throws; free points that we just throw away or we take advantage of. Bonuses that we miss because we choose wrong, or those that we make because we choose right. Life is all the things that will happen, regardless, in between that time on the line.

Often, you will be faced with opportunity. Sometimes it comes with risk, and no doubt a greater reward. On many occasions, you will feel yourself freeze up. Hesitate. Hesitation is natural, but how long you hesitate depends on you. In a matter of nanoseconds you start to decide what will you do. What seems like forever is only a short moment in your decision making process. Do you take the risk or lose the chance? You can't succeed unless you try. That means you have to take action!

Risk is the down payment for success. Muhammad Ali said that "he who is not courageous enough to take risks will accomplish nothing in life." We only regret the chances we didn't take, relationships we were afraid to have, and the decisions we waited too long to make.

One day a friend of mine, that goes by Don Chief, said "man you're too much of an opportunist." I replied, "I know. How else will I know if it's going to work out?" I feel that I would rather be 0-5 versus 0-0. The 0-5 record gives me the experience to become better. Sharpen my skills. I at least took the chance. Through my experience, I have the opportunity to learn the lesson in the loss. There is no triumph without trying.

The greatest mistake you can make in life is to continually fearing you will make one.

There's a fine line between success and failure; and I'm willing to challenge it every day. If I'm right, I'm a genius. If I'm wrong, I get to start over.

Phillip Williams, a high school and college friend of mine, and I were having a discussion. He was telling me about how he wanted to venture away from teaching in the classroom setting, and begin teaching private music lessons. Phil is super educated with many degrees and certifications that he felt he needed before he ventured out. To me, it sounded like excuses made to not get out of his comfort zone. As I sat and listened to him, I heard the fear and hesitation in his voice. I said, "Man!!...Damn!!!....you're dribbling too much, just shoot the shot!!" What I meant by that was…how long was he going to spend getting ready before he ever goes for his dreams. He was overly prepared. I understand education is the key to preparation. And the glorious day that preparation meets opportunity is success, but there is an action needed when it does. I told him to stop being scared and shoot his shot. I said, "you miss 100% of the shots you don't take!!" He brought up a few of my failures, and I brought up the success that came after. I told him, "My thought process doesn't have fear attached to it!! Yours does!!" He was a bit unsettled, but the truth is what it is.

In the game of basketball, if you shoot a shot and miss….guess what?!?! A rebound is available. If you are willing

33. You Miss 100% Of The Shots You Don't Take

to grab your own rebound and put the shot back up so you can score, it's definitely better than never shooting a shot or getting in the game at all. Your journey to success will present the same opportunities.

John F. Kennedy said, "There are risks and costs to action. But they are far less than the long range risks of comfortable inaction."

My parting advice to you is….SHOOT THE SHOT!!!!!

YOU DON'T HAVE TO BE GREAT
TO START.
BUT YOU HAVE TO GET STARTED
TO BE GREAT.

-LES BROWN-

34. The Fortune Is In The Follow Through

Have you ever noticed that when a batter is at bat in a baseball game, the pitch comes, he connects, and then follows through with the swing.....and all of a sudden!!!...HOME RUN!!! Or what about in a basketball game, the shooter is deep in 3 point territory, steps up, shoots the shot, perfect form, arch, and an amazing follow through with the shot....then SWISH!!!!! Or maybe even you watch football; the quarterback drops back, the receiver is going deep, 50 yards down the field and counting....and the quarterback launches the ball in the air with the most gracious follow through...and TOUCHDOWN!!!!

Whether it was the HOME RUN, SWISH, or TOUCHDOWN; they all required a follow through. Without the follow through, each would have fallen short. That's exactly what happens to us when we don't do that particular action needed in life. We fall short. We miss.

Some of the best sales advice I ever got was just that. The fortune is in the follow through. There is so much left unaccomplished just because someone doesn't follow through. That's what closing the deal is about.

You will have goals in life that you have to revisit, and follow through on. They will not complete themselves. If you throw your ideas, dreams, goals, and vision in the air with no follow through; eventually, they will drop flat.

Focus on the process of closing, perseverance, and dedication.

LUCKY BY CHOICE

There was a very, very, very dear friend of mine named Weslyn "Mama Wes" Monroe. A legend in her own right, she was the mother of the also dearly departed legend, late, great hip-hop/country rap tunes, musical icon...Pimp C of UGK. She had this made-up word that she used to use...."stick-to-it-ness". She used to say, "That's all you need to succeed in life or the music business. If you stick with it long enough, eventually you will get it right." As crazy as it sounds, she was right. If you keep following through, and attempting to make the shot or close the deal; you will see some success.

Not that this concept needs anymore explanation, but I want to "follow through" with this. On this journey, you must finish strong. Each milestone, each goal will require that you not only start your plans; but you must complete them, in order to see the success that you seek.

If it is indeed for you, the fortune is in the follow through.

YOU NEVER KNOW HOW CLOSE YOU ARE......

NEVER GIVE UP ON YOUR DREAMS!!!

35. Lose Yourself

*"If you had one shot or one opportunity
to seize everything you ever wanted in one moment;
Would you capture it or just let it slip?"*

*"You better lose yourself in the music, the moment
You own it, you better never let it go;
You only get one shot, do not miss your chance to blow,
This opportunity comes once in a lifetime……"*

Those were two excerpts from one of my favorite songs, "Lose Yourself", by Eminem; an international icon, multi-platinum, award winning rapper, entertainer, record producer, and actor. In my opinion, that song is the epitome of determination, competition, and passion.

I met a guy named Brain Nieves in 2016. He said, "life is a daring bold adventure, or it's nothing at all." He also said that, "you have to be a heat seeking missile for success." Two super, powerful statements about the state of mind you must possess in order to accomplish greatness in life.

I share a belief with my fraternity brothers that one must be thoroughly immersed to enjoy the true spirit of something. Lukewarm enthusiasm is unacceptable.

I saw a jaw-dropping statement one day by Grant Cardone. It said, "Become obsessed about the things you want. Otherwise, you are going to spend a lifetime being obsessed with making up excuses as to why you didn't get the life you wanted." All I could say was wow. Imagine that, if you put in the time and energy to get what you want today, you won't have to find the time and energy to deal with what you don't want tomorrow.

As I've stated before, I've gone through some tough times in my lifetime; many of which I felt all I had left was myself. People ask me how did I survive and make it through those phases. What drove me? I tell them, I was tuned in to my star player. I survived because the fire inside me burned brighter than the fire around me.

I allowed myself to get lost within my own greatness. Once I did, I was no longer lost. The world became clearer. I realized that everything I needed to achieve, I already had. I was looking for it around me, when all along, it was already in me.

Success is made from something deep down inside; a burning desire, a dream, a vision. You have to have the skill, and the will. But the will must be stronger than the skill.

Back to the title of the chapter and the song which inspired it; there is a central theme in "Lose Yourself" about seizing the moment. It's a cap on the frustrations, anxieties, and setbacks that everyone can relate to. Not everyone grew up as a poor rapper from Detroit, but it's Eminem's unmatched ability to impart raw emotion that gives him the credibility to put together an anthem that tells us to seize the day and live in the moment.

In Latin, seize the day is "carpe diem." The phrase is used to urge someone to make the most of the present time and give little thought to the future. Not that the future isn't important, but today is the right now.

With an *"I bet you didn't know this"* moment, I will close. In 1999, I committed to losing myself everyday in the quest for

35. Lose Yourself

success in each individual day. So much so, that I got two tattoos on that very day as a reminder and semi-public display of my mindset. One tattoo says "One Life To Live", and below it, the other says "One Day At A Time." Those two tattoos, together, give you the insight on how I view, approach, and conquer each day.

Today. Right now, I challenge you to
"Lose Yourself in the Giving of Yourself to Each Day."

36. Take Charge!

To take charge is defined as assuming control or responsibility. This chapter has no glorious story that will be told, with a moral victory explained at the end. This chapter was written, and very brief it is, as just a reminder. Below are 10 statements to simply encourage and remind you to, and how to take charge of your life.

1. Be proactive.
2. Develop a sense of urgency.
3. Take control or be controlled.
4. Opportunity doesn't go away.
   It just goes to the next person.
5. Take every chance. Drop every fear.
6. You can stand there thinking, "if only",
   or you can take charge and change it.
7. Don't wait for your ship to come in. Swim out to it.
8. Hope is not a strategy.
9. Be crazy enough to know you can do anything in life.
10. Take Charge, and don't apologize for it.

Remember the saying from Les Brown....."You don't have to be great to get started, but you have to get started to be great." Take the first step, and your mind will mobilize all of its forces to your aid. But the first essential is that you must take charge, and begin. Once you have taken charge, all that is within and without you will come to your assistance.

Everybody wants something, but not willing to do something until most times it's too late. Make a decision!! Do Something!! TAKE CHARGE!!

IT WILL HURT

IT WILL TAKE TIME

IT WILL REQUIRE DEDICATION

IT WILL REQUIRE WILLPOWER

YOU WILL NEED TO MAKE HEALTHY DECISIONS

IT REQUIRES SACRIFICE

YOU WILL NEED TO PUSH YOUR BODY TO ITS MAX

THERE WILL BE TEMPTATION

BUT I PROMISE YOU THIS

WHEN YOU REACH YOUR GOAL

IT WILL HAVE BEEN

WORTH IT

37. Ordinary vs EXTRA-Ordinary

I can't remember where I heard or read it first, but it was some time ago. I now use it as a riddle when speaking to people as a motivational speaker, life coach, consultant, or just in everyday conversation.

"What is the difference between ordinary and extraordinary?" That's the question I would ask them. You wouldn't believe the answers I've gotten over the years. Although none of them are wrong, most people assume I'm looking for a really complicated, intellectual, or philosophical answer. The simple truth is that the difference is the "extra." That's it. The extra.

Ordinary people believe only in the possible. Extraordinary people visualize not what is possible or probable, but rather what is impossible. And by visualizing the impossible, they begin to see it as possible and make it so. They set out to do ordinary things in an extraordinary way.

To me, ordinary is way too easy. There's no challenge or pride in it for me. You have to pay your dues. It costs something to be extraordinary. Once you get out of that place of ordinary, and experience extraordinary, you will never go back. Your memory won't let you.

In 2011, I took the time to read a book titled "The 33 Strategies of War" by Robert Greene. He's the critically acclaimed author of "The 48 Laws of Power", "The Art of Seduction", and "Mastery". All are bestsellers.

In that book, Strategy 24 is to "Take The Line Of Least Expectation: The Ordinary-Extraordinary Strategy." It says, "People expect your behavior to conform to known patterns and conventions. Your task as a strategist is to upset their expectations. First do something ordinary and conventional to fix their image of you, then hit them with the extraordinary. Sometimes the ordinary is extraordinary because it is unexpected."

That notion leads me to a concept that I practice in life, and in business. I love to under promise, and over deliver. The impact and fascination you receive from your results will always be extraordinary. For example, if you ask me to help you move 50 boxes out of 80 that you need to move before 5pm. I'll commit to moving maybe 30 of the boxes before that time. All the while, I know that I'm capable of moving all 80 before 2pm. I won't tell you that I'm going to do it. I'll just go over and beyond your expectation and do it, and when you see the result…..all you see is something extraordinary. You will then perceive and treat me as such.

Ordinary people just talk about their dreams and never take action to accomplish them. Extraordinary people are 100% committed to their dreams and are willing to do whatever it takes to make them come true. The true difference is the standards of them. Extraordinary people continue to raise their standards. Ordinary people are typically content with average and mediocre.

My advice to you, if you want to continue to be extraordinary, is to change your "should-list" to a "must-list". When you change the things you think you should do, to the things you must do; you will see the elevation from ordinary to extraordinary.

37. Ordinary vs EXTRA-Ordinary

Without being too verbose, the only way I know to close this chapter is with an extraordinary quote from Martin Luther King, Jr.

"Whatever your life's work is, do it well. A man should do his job so well that the living, the dead, and the unborn could do it no better."

DON'T QUIT

WHEN THINGS GO WRONG, AS THEY SOMETIMES WILL,
WHEN THE ROAD YOU'RE TRUDGING SEEMS ALL UPHILL,
WHEN THE FUNDS ARE LOW AND DEBTS ARE HIGH,
AND YOU WANT TO SMILE BUT HAVE TO SIGH.
WHEN CARE IS PRESSING YOU DOWN A BIT,
REST, IF YOU MUST, BUT DON'T YOU QUIT.

LIFE IS QUEER WITH ITS TWISTS AND TURNS,
AS EVERYONE OF US SOMETIMES LEARNS,
AND MANY A FAILURE TURNS ABOUT,
WHEN HE MIGHT HAVE WON IF HE'D STUCK IT OUT,
DON'T GIVE UP THOUGH THE PACE SEEMS SLOW,
YOU MIGHT SUCCEED WITH ANOTHER BLOW.

OFTEN THE STRUGGLER HAS GIVEN UP,
WHEN HE MIGHT CAPTURED THE VICTOR'S CUP.
AND HE LEARNED TOO LATE, WHEN THE NIGHT SLIPPED DOWN,
HOW CLOSE HE WAS TO THE GOLDEN CROWN,

SUCCESS IS FAILURE TURNED INSIDE OUT,
THE SILVER TINT OF CLOUDS OF DOUBT,
AND YOU NEVER CAN TELL HOW CLOSE YOU ARE,
IT MAY BE NEAR WHEN IT SEEMS AFAR,
SO STICK TO THE FIGHT WHEN YOU'RE HARDEST HIT,
IT'S WHEN THINGS SEEM WORST THAT YOU MUSTN'T QUIT.

38. Do It Again

We often hear from successful people that failure is an inevitable stepping stone on the way to accomplishing our goals.

But how many failures does it take to reach success?

Well, for the Rocket Chemical Company, now known as the WD-40 Company, the answer was 39.

In 1953, in a small lab in San Diego, California, Norm Larsen, founder of the fledgling Rocket Chemical Company, and his staff of three set out to create a line of rust-prevention solvents and degreasers for use in the aerospace industry.

It took them 40 attempts to get their water displacing formula to work, but on the 40th attempt, they got it right in a big way. WD-40 was born. WD-40 stands for Water Displacement, 40th formula. That's the name straight out of the lab book used by the chemist who developed the product.

By now, you definitely know that I hold the number 40 dear to my heart; so it was only right that I tell you about another story of a significant 40.

Norm and his crew are the epitome of persistence and repetition. They proved that, if paired with a good idea, perseverance through failure can bring great success. Practice made perfect. I wonder how many people can say that they would have stuck it out through 39 failures.

LUCKY BY CHOICE

This chapter is all about persistence and repetition. Doing it again, and again, and again, and again, until you see the growth, progress, and/or success.

We've often heard, probably from Malcolm Gladwell's book Outliers, that 10,000 hours is the magic number to make someone an expert. Or maybe you've heard that it takes 21 days to make or break a habit. Whether it's 10,000 hours or 21 days, persistence and repetition of an action will guide you to success.

Calvin Coolidge, the 30th President of the United States, said that "Nothing in this world can take the place of persistence. Talent will not; nothing is more common than unsuccessful people with talent. Genius will not; unrewarded genius is almost a proverb. Education will not; the world is full of educated derelicts. Persistence and determination alone are omnipotent. The slogan "Press On" has solved and always will solve the problems of the human race."

As a river cuts through rock, not because of its power, but because of its persistence; I encourage you to try, try, and try again. Stop letting trying to be perfect postpone your progress. If you fail, just as Norm Larsen and his staff did 39 times, try again.

39. Who Gave You The Right To Quit?

It's no secret that I feel that Muhammad Ali was one of the greatest motivational icons ever. He once said, "I hated every minute of training," but then told himself "Don't quit. Suffer now, and live the rest of your life as a champion."

We all have those moments in time when it seems that the load gets too heavy, or we can't see the light at the end of the tunnel, or we just get tired. All of those are real and natural occurrences. It is at that time we have to remind ourselves of our why. What's our reason for wanting to do better? Who's our reason for wanting to do better? What's our purpose in life?

Nobody ever said it would be easy, but I can guarantee that going after your goals and dreams will be worth it. That sense of accomplishment and fulfillment you feel is priceless. There's nothing like the feeling of winning.

The most intense fight a human will ever have is between the person they are and the person they are becoming. You are your toughest competition and critic. Every day, your goal should be to outdo yesterday's you. That won't be easy. You will have your good days and your bad days. But don't you quit.

Quitting is not an option when winning is your goal. You've heard the old Vince Lombardi saying, "Winners never quit, and quitters never win." You aren't defeated when you lose, you are defeated when you quit! You may be knocked down, but not knocked out. Get up and fight. You may fall 99 times, but as long as you get up 100 times, you are still winning.

LUCKY BY CHOICE

There's a poem by Langston Hughes titled Mother To Son that I'd like to share with you. Hughes wrote it when he was 21 years old. He structures the poem as a conversation between a Mother and her Son. The Mother begins by telling her Son how hard her life has been. The Mother describes the challenges in her life using symbols like tacks, splinters, uncarpeted floor, and dark, unlit corners. She encourages her Son not to turn back, because she never will. By using the metaphor of the staircase, Hughes alludes to Jacob's Ladder. The Mother character is on a difficult and challenging uphill journey, hoping that if she endures her struggles she can eventually reach her goal. The Mother tries to help her Son maintain his faith as well, which will help him persevere through life's struggles. Without further ado.......*Mother To Son*.

Well, son, I'll tell you:
Life for me ain't been no crystal stair.
It's had tacks in it,
And splinters,
And boards torn up,
And places with no carpet on the floor —
Bare.
But all the time
I'se been a-climbin' on,
And reachin' landin's,
And turnin' corners,
And sometimes goin' in the dark
Where there ain't been no light.
So boy, don't you turn back.
Don't you set down on the steps
'Cause you finds it's kinder hard.
Don't you fall now —
For I'se still goin', honey,
I'se still climbin',
And life for me ain't been no crystal stair.

39. Who Gave You The Right To Quit

Life will not always be fair, nor will it be easy. Hughes motivates his readers to never falter in the face of life's challenges. This means if she can overcome everything that she has been through; then her Son shouldn't stop and quit because life is hard. The Mother wouldn't give her Son the right to quit. So who gave you the right to quit?

I have a question to ask you before I close. Remember that guy that gave up?.............Me neither. Nobody ever does.

Part Four:

SUCCESS IS A JOURNEY, NOT A DESTINATION

40. Chance Favors The Prepared Mind

In the 1995 movie starring Steven Seagal, *Under Seige 2: Dark Territory*, I remembered a quote said and wrote it down. That was the first time the quote "Chance Favors The Prepared Mind" caught my attention. Sometime thereafter, years actually, I decided to do some research on the meaning. Even though I had my own interpretation of it, I wanted to see what others had to say. Mind you, in 1995 the internet was a baby, and I was a foreigner to its operations. I barely knew how to use email. So my research didn't begin until about 5 years later.

On December 7, 1854, as dean of the brand new Faculty of Sciences at Lille, Louis Pasteur gave the opening speech in which he said, *"in the fields of observation, chance only favours the mind which is prepared..."* By this he meant that sudden flashes of insight don't just happen — they are the products of preparation. Preparation, therefore, is the key to a successful and fulfilling life. Louis Pasteur's statement was not only a scientifically clever phrase, it was a principle that would define his career. The quote is a wonderful nugget of wisdom that reminds me that I must stay observant and open to creative opportunities and solutions.

Luck isn't some mystical energy that dances around the universe randomly bestowing people with satisfaction and joy.......You create your own luck. Luck is what happens when preparation meets opportunity. Preparation is defined as the action or process of making ready or being made ready for use or consideration. Opportunity is defined as a set of circumstances that makes it possible to do something.

When preparation meets opportunity, success is inevitable.

Benjamin Franklin said, "by failing to prepare, you are preparing to fail." If you do not get your thoughts, resources, and plans in alignment with your goals; you will not see success. You have to create a plan to carry out your desires. Planning is being able to look into the future, bring it into the present, and do something about it now. Knowing what you want the end result to be allows you to prepare your plan better. You begin with the end in mind.

When I was on line and pledging my fraternity in college, we were given a phrase called the 12 P's.

> *"Proper planning prevents piss poor performance, and piss poor performance prevents punishment and pain!!"*

The message was that if we prepared ahead of time for the things we knew we had to do in the future, we would be in a better position for success when that time and opportunity came. If we didn't, we suffered the unpleasant consequences and repercussions of failure.

I have one simple message for you as I close this chapter.........Prepare yourself in every way you can by increasing your knowledge and adding to your experience, so that you can make the most of opportunity when it occurs. Remember, opportunity doesn't go away, it just goes to someone else. Don't get caught being unprepared when opportunity comes knocking on your door. Prepare to receive what you want.

In the famous words of Malcolm X, *"the future belongs to those who prepare for it today."*

41. Are We There Yet?

It's been said, and very true, that a journey of a million miles starts with one step. More importantly, you need to know where those million miles will take you. Too often in life, people will set out on a course to go somewhere with no directions, no map, no nothing. Getting lost is guaranteed.

In this chapter, I want to highlight some facts about planning a journey and the patience it requires. Let me ask you this. Have you ever gone on a road trip with no map or directions on how to get there? How did that work for you? Let me tell you what will happen if you don't have a map or directions......You won't know how much progress you have made. You won't know how much time you have left to arrive. You won't know if you're going in the right direction. You won't know if you've ever arrived. You may not ever make it to your destination at all. You will just be moving, probably fast, like a hamster on a wheel.

Direction is much more important than speed, and many are going nowhere fast.

To prevent yourself from being the hamster on the wheel going nowhere fast, let's look at our journeys in the proper perspective. First, accept the fact that there is no finish line in success. So be prepared to constantly strive for different milestones and levels of success. Second, in order to get from point A to point B, you have to establish the relativity and relevance between the two. Make sure that you are traveling with efficiency in mind. Make sure each step you take have connected goals. It would be a shame if you jumped all over the place, and had no order to your steps. Third, you must be patient. Don't count the days, make the days count. Be sure that you are getting the most out of each day and each step you take. Fourth, John Bytheway said, "inch by inch, anything's a cinch…..yard by yard, life's hard." My interpretation of that statement is to embrace the step by step process. It's easier than trying to do it in leaps and bounds. The step by step process is the foundation of any map or set of directions. Last, life should be a thrilling and exhilarating journey. Don't let not having a plan or map or directions have you frustrated on your journey and always wondering "where am I?" or "are we there yet?"

If you're walking down the right path, with a plan, a map, and specific directions on when, what, how, why, and where to go; and you're willing to keep walking, eventually you'll make progress and achieve success.

My last morsel of advice to you is to enjoy the journey, not just the destination.

42. There Is No Plan B

It was the year 1519 and Hernán Cortés, with some 600 Spaniards, 16 or so horses and 11 boats, had landed on a vast inland plateau called, Mexico.

The Spanish conquistador and his men were about to embark on a conquest of an empire that hoarded some of the world's greatest treasure. Gold, silver and precious Aztec jewels were just some of what this treasure had to offer anyone who succeeded in their quest to obtain it.

But, with only 600 men — none of whom had encumbered themselves with protective armour – conquering an empire so extensive in its territories could only be undertaken by a man with a death wish.

This daring undertaking was made even more insurmountable by the fact that for more than 600 years, conquerors with far more resources at their disposal who attempted to colonize the Yucatan Peninsula, never succeeded. Hernán Cortés was well-aware of this fact. And it was for this reason, that he took a different approach when he landed on the land of the Mayans.

Instead of charging through cities and forcing his men into immediate battle, Hernán Cortés stayed on the beach and awoke the souls of his men with melodious cadences – in the form of emblazoned speeches.

His speeches were ingeniously designed to urge on the spirit of adventure and invoke the thirst of lifetimes of fortune amongst his troops. His orations bore fruit, for what was

LUCKY BY CHOICE

supposedly a military exploit, now bore the appearance of extravagant romance in the imaginations of Cortés' troops.

But, ironically, it would only just be 3 words which Cortés' murmured, that would change the history of the New World. As they marched inland to face their enemies, Cortés ordered, "BURN THE BOATS!!!"

It was a decision that should have backfired. For if Cortés and his men were on the brink of defeat, there wasn't an exit strategy in place to save their lives. Remarkably though, the command to burn the boats had an opposite effect on his men because now, they were left with only 2 choices — die, or ensure victory. And fight they did.

We know today, how Cortés' decision to burn his boats panned out. Hernán Cortés became the first man in 600 years to successfully conquer Mexico.

In Sun Tzu's "The Art of War", it brings to light the logic behind the decisions of history's greatest conquerors to burn their boats at the risk of being killed in enemy hands. It was simply to eradicate any notion of retreat from the minds of their troops and commit themselves unwaveringly to the cause – VICTORY. Defeat wasn't an option at all. THERE WAS NO PLAN B.

Hopefully, that story has your attention and has tapped into a special place in your warrior's spirit. Your vision, dreams, and goals should never come with a plan B. I'm not saying not to have multiple goals, but I am saying do not settle for less than you want regarding a specific goal. Don't get going, and when the going gets tough, you decide to turn away. You have to be committed, dedicated, and passionate about your goals in life. I'm saying FAILURE IS NOT AN OPTION!!

42. There Is No Plan B

Again, let me be clear here. Many people equate success with money and financial resources. So let me say this. You have many and residual bills, so you should have many and residual incomes. The research says that most millionaires have at least 7 streams of income. Please, please, please understand this…….those millionaires also have at least 7 Plan A's. THERE IS NO PLAN B!!!

As I close, let's agree that you will face some challenges and obstacles in life. The mindset you adopt while facing that adversity will declare whether you are victorious or not. Just like Hernán Cortés, you will have to take away the safety net to guarantee yourself that you go all the way. Remove your training wheels and handicaps in your life. Allow no comfort zones that you can retreat to. Not saying that you must, but it's one hell of an incentive if you BURN THE BOATS!!

SUCCESS IN LIFE COMES WHEN YOU SIMPLY REFUSE TO GIVE UP, WITH GOALS SO STRONG THAT OBSTACLES, FAILURE, AND LOSS ONLY ACT AS MOTIVATION.

43. Location, Location, Location

One of the best coaches I've ever had in my entire life was named Robert Woods. He was the Head Football Coach at my high school, Wilmer-Hutchins. He taught me many great things about football. Even more, through football, he taught me a lot about life. We used to have a training session in football practice called "Alignment Period." In this section of practice we would simply just line up in the position we were playing according to the play called, make sure we were starting out in the right place, and knew where we should go from that place. It wasn't even full speed. We would literally just walk through the play, to make sure everyone knew where to start from and where to end up. Back then, outside of football, it didn't have as much impact in life as it does now.

Just like in real estate, it was "location, location, location." I eventually realized that the job of a coach is to put the players and the team in the best position (location) to win together. Coach Woods' focus on our alignment was one of the reasons he was so successful at leading us to a State Championship and many successful seasons.

To this day, I believe that being in the right place, at the right time is all about positioning and alignment. For the most part, you just have to be there to give yourself a chance to win. "Show Up and Show Out!!" is what I've been taught.

Many times, you may not have a coach that will be available to put you in position. So you must learn to put yourself in position. With the younger generation, you hear a lot of them say "put me on." Meaning they want someone to hand them an opportunity. Some may be well deserving, and some may not.

My advice has always been to put yourself in position, "put yourself on." Don't wait on or expect someone to give you the opportunity and keys to success and "put you on" just because you asked.

Opportunity doesn't always come when, how, where, and in what form you prefer. You must be able to recognize it, and more importantly, be in position and prepared to claim it.

Ray Kroc, founder of McDonald's, said "The two requirements for major success are being in the right place at the right time, and doing something about it."

Ironically, a lot of us don't realize that McDonald's isn't really a burger-flipping restaurant chain. Well, it is, but not purely. Peel back the layers and you'll find that the corporate entity is actually one hell of a real estate company. Former McDonald's CFO, Harry J. Sonneborn, is even quoted as saying, "we are not technically in the food business. We are in the real estate business. The only reason we sell fifteen-cent hamburgers is because they are the greatest producer of revenue, from which our tenants can pay us our rent."

Instead of making money by selling supplies to franchisees or demanding huge royalties…the McDonald's Corporation became the landlord to its franchisees. They bought the properties and then leased them out – at large markups. In addition to that regular income, the corporation would take a percentage of each location's gross sales.

Today, McDonald's makes its money on real estate through two methods. Its real estate subsidiary will buy and sell hot properties while also collecting rents on each of its franchised locations. McDonald's restaurants are in over 100 countries and have probably served over 100 billion hamburgers. There are

43. Location, Location, Location

over 36,000 locations worldwide, of which only 15% are owned and operated by the McDonald's corporation directly. The rest are franchisee-operated.

So see, even in the success of the leading hamburger business, it's all about "location, location, location." No matter what your goals and dreams are, your positioning and alignment (your location) must be well thought out. Just as Ray Kroc did with McDonald's, you must do with yourself. Put yourself in the right place, at the right time; and do something about it.

IT IS NOT THE CRITIC WHO COUNTS
NOT THE MAN WHO POINTS OUT HOW THE STRONG MAN STUMBLES
OR WHERE THE DOER OF DEEDS COULD HAVE DONE BETTER
THE CREDIT BELONGS TO THE MAN
WHO IS ACTUALLY IN THE ARENA
WHOSE FACE IS MARRED
BY DUST AND SWEAT AND BLOOD
WHO STRIVES VALIANTLY
WHO ERRS AND COMES UP SHORT AGAIN AND AGAIN
BECAUSE THERE IS NO EFFORT
WITHOUT ERROR OR SHORTCOMING
BUT WHO KNOWS THE GREAT ENTHUSIASMS
THE GREAT DEVOTIONS
WHO SPENDS HIMSELF FOR A WORTHY CAUSE
WHO, AT THE BEST, KNOWS, IN THE END
THE TRIUMPH OF HIGH ACHIEVEMENT
AND WHO, AT THE WORST, IF HE FAILS
AT LEAST HE FAILS WHILE DARING GREATLY
SO THAT HIS PLACE SHALL NEVER BE
WITH THOSE COLD AND TIMID SOULS WHO KNEW NEITHER
VICTORY NOR DEFEAT

44. The Law Of The Harvest

You know the sayings so, so well. You will reap what you sow!! What goes around comes around. That is the premise behind the Law of the Harvest. Simply stated, the Law of the Harvest says that in life, we will reap what we sow; we will reap more than we sow; and we will reap later than we sow. Good choices, like seeds, ultimately bring forth good fruit as a reward. Bad choices, like bad seeds, ultimately bring bad fruit as a consequence. The Law of the Harvest is applicable in every area of life—marriage, parenting, business, family relationships, finances, and more. We can't choose when to apply its principles; it is in operation all the time. Therefore, we must constantly be mindful of the seeds we sow. Once we've sown, we can't change the harvest. You can't have a harvest without a few weeds either. It's part of the process.

There's no strength like the strength and character it takes to still yourself and apply the personal discipline it takes to allow yourself to be completely processed by life and by the consequences of your own choices.

The power of process is absolutely extraordinary. People misunderstand and devalue the power of process. We think that we can outsmart and outrun process and still get what we want. When in fact, it is impossible to do so. You have to fall in love with the process of becoming great. Embrace the evolution that the process provides.

Just as a caterpillar evolves to a butterfly; a tadpole to a frog; and coal to a diamond; you will evolve as well. But you have to respect, embrace, and don't cheat the process. Success is a process. You must be patient and tolerant.

The Law of the Harvest is similar to the process of baking a cake. When baking a cake, it will call for certain ingredients. Once you have the ingredients, you can't just put them all in and mix them up at the same time; or you just might not end up with a cake at all. You can't skip the steps of the recipe, because the ingredients go in a certain order. There is a certain amount of each ingredient needed, then a certain amount of time to let it process. If anything is done out of order, or prematurely, you will be sure to not get the expected results.

So in understanding the Law of the Harvest, and reaping what you sow; know that if you plant honesty, you will reap trust. If you plant friendliness, you will reap friends. If you plant integrity, you will reap respect. If you plant perseverance, you will reap victory. If you plant hard work, you will reap success. If you plant dedication, you will reap excellence.

But......

If you plant dishonesty, you will reap distrust. If you plant selfishness, you will reap loneliness. If you plant laziness, you will reap stagnation. If you plant bitterness, you will reap isolation. If you plant greed, you will reap loss. If you plant gossip, you will reap enemies. If you plant worries, you will reap wrinkles.

I want to leave you with an incredible, inspirational short story that I read some time ago, titled The Emperor and The Seed.

An emperor in the Far East was growing old and knew it was time to choose his successor. Instead of choosing one of his assistants or his children, he decided something different. He called young people in the kingdom together one day. He said,

44. The Law Of The Harvest

"It is time for me to step down and choose the next emperor. I have decided to choose one of you."

The kids were shocked! But the emperor continued. "I am going to give each one of you a seed today. One very special seed. I want you to plant the seed, water it and come back here after one year from today with what you have grown from this one seed. I will then judge the plants that you bring, and the one I choose will be the next emperor!"

One boy named Ling was there that day and he, like the others, received a seed. He went home and excitedly told his mother the story. She helped him get a pot and planting soil, and he planted the seed and watered it carefully. Every day he would water it and watch to see if it had grown. After about three weeks, some of the other youths began to talk about their seeds and the plants that were beginning to grow. Ling kept checking his seed, but nothing ever grew. 3 weeks, 4 weeks, 5 weeks went by. Still nothing. By now, others were talking about their plants but Ling didn't have a plant, and he felt like a failure. Six months went by, still nothing in Ling's pot. He just knew he had killed his seed.

Everyone else had trees and tall plants, but he had nothing. Ling didn't say anything to his friends, however. He just kept waiting for his seed to grow.

A year finally went by and all the youths of the kingdom brought their plants to the emperor for inspection. Ling told his mother that he wasn't going to take an empty pot. But honest about what happened, Ling felt sick to his stomach, but he knew his mother was right. He took his empty pot to the palace. When Ling arrived, he was amazed at the variety of plants grown by the other youths. They were beautiful in all shapes and sizes. Ling put his empty pot on the floor and many of the other kinds laughed at him. A few felt sorry for him and just said, "Hey nice try."

When the emperor arrived, he surveyed the room and greeted the young people. Ling just tried to hide in the back. "What great plants, trees and flowers you have grown," said the emperor. "Today, one of you will be appointed the next emperor!" All of a sudden, the emperor spotted Ling at the back of the room with his empty pot. He ordered his guards to bring him to the front. Ling was terrified. "The emperor knows I'm a failure! Maybe he will have me killed!"

When Ling got to the front, the Emperor asked his name. "My name is Ling," he replied. All the kids were laughing and making fun of him. The emperor asked everyone to quiet down. He looked at Ling, and then announced to the crowd, "Behold your new emperor! His name is Ling!" Ling couldn't believe it. Ling couldn't even grow his seed. How could he be the new emperor? Then the emperor said, "One year ago today, I gave everyone here a seed. I told you to take the seed, plant it, water it, and bring it back to me today. But I gave you all boiled seeds, which would not grow. All of you, except Ling, have brought me trees and plants and flowers. When you found that the seed would not grow, you substituted another seed for the one I gave you. Ling was the only one with the courage and honesty to bring me a pot with my seed in it. Therefore, he is the one who will be the new emperor!"

Let the inspirational words of wisdom in this short story remind you to be careful of what you plant now. It will determine what you will reap tomorrow. The seeds you now scatter, will make life worse or better; either your life or the ones who will come after. Yes, someday, you will enjoy the fruits, or you will pay for the choices you plant today.

FOR A SEED TO GROW,
IT MUST NOT ONLY BE COVERED IN DIRT,
IT MUST PUSH THROUGH THE DIRT
TO ULTIMATELY SPROUT.
IT'S THE SAME FOR US
AS WE PURSUE OUR GOALS.
YOU HAVE TO BE WILLING TO
PUSH THROUGH YOUR "DIRT".
TO PUSH THROUGH THE CHALLENGES,
SETBACKS, FAILURES OR
HAVING TO START OVER.
DON'T GIVE UP BECAUSE IT GETS HARD.
JUST KEEP PUSHING SO YOUR SEED CAN GROW.

45. The Bridge Builder

An old man going a lone highway,
Came, at the evening cold and gray.
To a chasm vast and deep and wide.
Through which was flowing a sullen tide.

The old man crossed in the twilight dim,
The sullen stream had no fear for him;
But he turned when safe on the other side
And built a bridge to span the tide.

"Old man," said a fellow pilgrim near,
"You are wasting your strength with building here;
Your journey will end with the ending day,
You never again will pass this way;
You've crossed the chasm, deep and wide,
Why build this bridge at evening tide?"

The builder lifted his old gray head;
"Good friend, in the path I have come," he said,
"There followeth after me today,
A youth whose feet must pass this way.

This chasm that has been as naught to me,
To that fair-haired youth may a pitfall be;
He, too, must cross in the twilight dim;
Good friend, I am building this bridge for him!"

That is a poem written by Will Allen Dromgoole titled *The Bridge Builder*, published in the early 1900's. It has a very clear message. It is about building a way for the future, and passing the torch along for the next generation. While that is definitely the sentiment I share through interpretation as well, I want to add a brief perspective to it.

It is my belief that we all play a key part in the development of our society. We must know our roles in it. Some of us are awesome visionaries. Some of us are skilled executioners. Some are both. Either way, we have a responsibility to know which part we must play at the right time in order to guarantee our own success, and the shared success of others.

In the poem, the old man was both a visionary and executioner. He had enough foresight and experience in life to know that a fair-haired youth will travel that same path. As an executioner, he was able to build a bridge that will allow the next generation to cross that way with some degree of ease.

On our journey to whatever we personally define as success, we will cross a bridge that someone built for us. It is our human and social responsibility to do the same when we encounter a new pitfall; that someday someone after us will have to cross. I challenge you to become The Bridge Builder.

STOP GETTING DISTRACTED BY THINGS THAT HAVE NOTHING TO DO WITH YOUR GOALS.

46. Write Out Loud!

A dream written down with a date becomes a goal. A goal broken down into steps becomes a plan. A plan backed by action makes your dreams come true. This chapter is about goal setting and bringing life to your ideas, goals, and dreams. I used to say, *"if it ain't on paper, it ain't real."* Now I know that doesn't apply to everything, but in this case, I'm pretty sure you can grasp the idea.

Take me for instance, I've had the idea to write this book for a very long time. In the beginning, it was just that, an idea. Then I began to take notes of my ideas. That made it real. Then I started to outline my thoughts and bring some sort of structure to it. After that, I was able to add more thoughts in the proper place, because on paper I created some order and a plan. Now here you are reading chapter 46 of an idea I decided to *"Write Out Loud!"*

One of the beautiful things about writing things down, for me at least, is that I don't have to remember anything. I prefer to let the paper remember everything, instead of me and my brain. I need to use my brain for other things. I'd rather a short pencil over a bad memory any day of the week.

Writing things out from your brain and onto paper gives you the opportunity to bring some clarity to your ideas. You are then able to look at what you have been thinking, and decide if it makes sense or not. You're able to develop those ideas and set proper goals to accompany them.

The definition of goal setting is the process of identifying something that you want to accomplish and establishing measurable goals and timeframes. Setting goals gives you long-term vision and short-term motivation. It focuses your acquisition of knowledge, and helps you to organize your time and your resources so that you can make the very most of your life. There is a strong correlation between self-motivation, personal goals and achievement. In order to get properly motivated, and indeed to achieve, it helps to spend some time thinking about your personal goals and what you want to achieve in your life.

Dr. Edwin Locke and Dr. Gary Latham spent many years researching the theory of goal setting, during which time they identified five elements that need to be in place for us to achieve our goals. According to Locke and Latham, there are five goal setting principles that can improve our chances of success:

1. *Clarity*
2. *Challenge*
3. *Commitment*
4. *Feedback*
5. *Task Complexity*

Let's look at each of these elements, and explore how you can apply them to your personal goals.

Clarity: When your goals are clear, you know what you're trying to achieve. You can also measure results accurately, and you know which behaviors to reward. However, when a goal is vague – or when you express it as a general instruction like "take initiative" – it isn't easy to measure, and it isn't motivating. You may not even know you've achieved it!

Challenge: People are often motivated by challenging goals, however it's important not to set a goal that is so challenging it

46. Write Out Loud!

can't be achieved. Develop self-discipline so that you have the persistence to work through problems.

Commitment: To be effective, your must understand your goals. Stay committed by using visualization techniques to imagine how your life will look once you've achieved your goal. Create a treasure map to remind yourself why you should work hard. Visual representations of your goal can help you stay committed, even when the going gets tough.

Feedback: In addition to selecting the right goals, you should also look for feedback, so that you can gauge how well you are progressing. Feedback gives you the opportunity to clarify your own expectations and adjust to the progression of your goals. Keep in mind that feedback doesn't have to come from other people. You can check how well you're doing by simply measuring your own progress.

Task Complexity: Take special care to ensure that work doesn't become too overwhelming when goals or assignments are highly complex. People who work in complicated and demanding roles can often push themselves too hard, if they don't take account of the complexity of the task.

Writing out our goals is something that many of us recognize as a vital part of achieving success. Goal setting leads to better performance by increasing motivation and efforts. Goals should be realistic and challenging. This gives an individual a feeling of pride and triumph when he attains them, and sets him up for the attainment of next goal. The more challenging the goal, the greater is the reward, generally; and the more is the passion for achieving it. Clear, particular and difficult goals are greater motivating factors than easy, general and vague goals.

LUCKY BY CHOICE

Now that you have the blueprint for setting your goals; write them down, organize them, and put a date on them. Then get busy living, or get busy dying. The decision belongs to you.

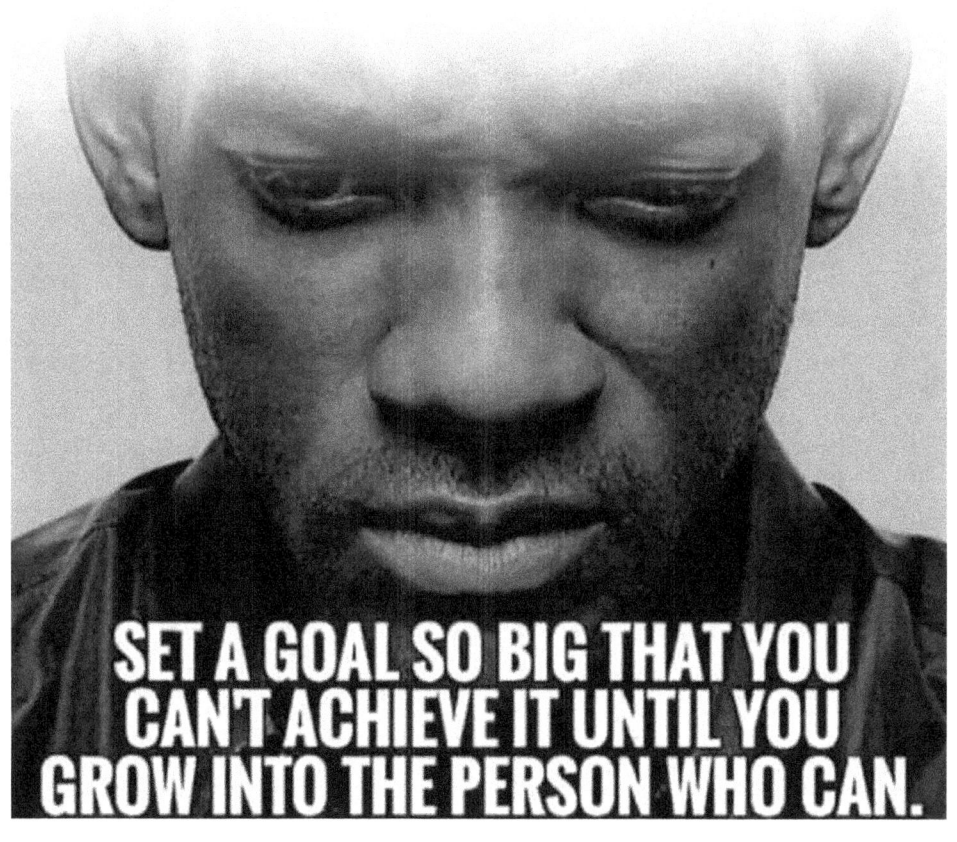

47. Staying Ready To Keep From Getting Ready

Stop getting ready to get ready!!! We always say what we want in life, but what happens when what we want arrives. Are we prepared to receive it? Or will we let poor preparation be the reason the opportunity passes us by. Opportunity doesn't go away, it just goes to the next person. I've missed out on some major things in life by not being ready.

The time was right, the stage was set…..and I was unprepared. By missing out, I truly learned that you must live your life preparing to accept, receive, and be able to give to the right opportunities when they present themselves……stay ready to keep from getting ready.

When you know what you want in life, you must learn to anticipate the opportunities that may come your way. How you prepare yourself for that will be key to your ability to attain certain levels of success. You must be able to recognize the type of opportunities that are directly related to your goals. It may not always come when, how, where, and in what form you prefer; but make no mistake about it, it will come, and you must already be conditioned for the opportunity.

The information that I wanted to give in this chapter is very brief, and very straight to the point. This is a very important thing to realize; that the chance to do something you really want to do can come when you least expect it. If you make yourself ready for anything that life throws at you, and be ready to embrace and experience it fully, you'll eventually seize your perfect opportunity to do something you want in life. Many people wait for years to 'catch their lucky break' and often when they finally get presented with an opportunity to do something incredible, they either;

1. Don't realize the opportunity is there.
2. Don't know how to react or,
3. They aren't ready.

And that's why sometimes it's good to just stay ready and be on the lookout for chances and ways to do something with your life. So make sure that every day, you're sharp, aware of yourself, and focused on what you want in life, and how you're going to get there. The thing to worry about is missing opportunities. It's always the things we don't do in life that we regret, so when the chance is there, and you see a gap or a moment where you could seize the day, just do it and think about it later. It either will be a good decision, or not, but you'll never know if you just don't' do it.

To laugh often and much,
to win the respect of intelligent people
and the affection of children,
to earn the appreciation of honest critics
and endure the betrayal of false friends;
to appreciate beauty,
to find the best in others,
to leave the world a bit better,
whether by a healthy child,
a garden patch,
or a redeemed social condition;
to know even one life has breathed easier
because you have lived,
this is to have succeeded.

RALPH WALDO EMERSON

48. Neither Should Be Wasted

The name of this chapter comes from a message I received from Jay-Z some years back, around 2004-2005 if I'm not mistaken. At that time I was the promoter for a mega-club in Dallas named Club Blue. I was doing some shows with a very famous radio personality named Greg Street. Well, one of our shows was with Uncle Luke of the 2 Live Crew. I picked him up from the airport, we made stops at a meet and greet/autograph signing at the YMCA, we went to eat, and back to the hotel before showtime. During that time, he said "man you're cool as hell, let me send you this invite to a pool party at a mansion in Miami." Now I'm thinking................OH MAN!!!....an Uncle Luke/2 Live Crew pool party!!!!....Sheesh!!!!.....I gotta thank Greg for this one. The night went well, and I stayed in contact with him and his brother Disco Rick for quite some time. Now let's get to the part about Jay-Z.

We all had Motorola Timeports back then, and that was how Luke sent the message to me. The invite list was an A-List of entertainers, and I felt super-privileged to be on the list. I noticed a name, Shawn Carter, and immediately knew who it was. I was working on starting my own magazine, and said to myself if I can get an interview from Jay-Z and launch my magazine with him on the cover.....I'll be in the game!!! So what did I do, I messaged him. Super proud of myself, and thinking I had favor; I asked him what it would take to get an interview from him and on the cover of my magazine......his reply was "a little bit of money, and a little bit of time; but neither should be wasted if you're not ready." And just like that, I left it alone. I had time, but no money. His phrase in his response is what inspired the name of this chapter.

Basically, I took at as him saying if you don't have the money; don't waste my time. All I could do was respect it. It forced me to start analyzing the value of my own time, and more importantly, the respect for others' time. I began to realize that time is so valuable because you can never get it back. Time is not replaceable, money is; but neither should be wasted. You can always make more money. You can't make more time. But again, neither should be wasted.

Many people can't see when they are wasting time, because they don't value it properly. In my opinion, time is more valuable than money. Time is so precious because you never know how much you have left. Research shows that 70 years is the average life span for human beings. That's 25,550 days…..the clock is ticking and you can't pause or rewind it.

Every morning you are handed 24 golden hours. They are one of the few things in this world that you get free of charge. If you had all the money in the world, you couldn't buy an extra hour. What will you do with this priceless treasure? Remember, you must use it, as it is given only once. Once wasted you cannot get it back.

Let's say that you have $86,400 in your account and someone stole $10 from you. Would you be upset and throw all of the $86,390 away in hopes of getting back at the person that took your $10? Or move on and live? Right, move on and live. See, we have 86,400 seconds in every day; so don't let someone's negative 10 seconds ruin the rest of the 86,390. Don't sweat the small stuff. Life is bigger than that. Make sure that you value and protect your time.

48. Neither Should Be Wasted

As I conclude, I want to share a quote from Malcolm X with you. He said, "In all our deeds, the proper value and respect for time determines success or failure."

My challenge to you is to stay focused on how you spend, value, and respect; money and time, but more importantly time. Neither should be wasted.

49. You Get What You Negotiate

Chester L. Karrass, the bestselling author of 'The Negotiating Game' and 'Give and Take', said that "In Business As In Life – You Don't Get What You Deserve, You Get What You Negotiate"; which also became a bestseller. In the book, he spoke about how to lay out step-by-step strategies for getting what you want by negotiating long term win-win relationships. This biggest thing I learned was how to prepare for a negotiation. The deal, or negotiation of it, can't be all about you. You must know everything the person you are negotiating with wants. Their needs come first. Why? Because if you can satisfy their needs, what reason would they have to say no? None. Now you have to make sure that your needs and wants out of the deal do not infringe too heavily upon theirs.

In Life, as it is in business, it's give and take. Understanding the other person's needs is just as important as knowing your own. What you argue or negotiate for, you get to keep. So don't approach life's negotiations arguing on behalf of your limitations. Ask for more than you expect, otherwise you may get less than you deserve.

This chapter is very brief, because I want you to focus on the meaning of the name of the chapter. So before I end, I want to share a poem with you from the book "Think and Grow Rich."

"I bargained with Life for a penny,
And Life would pay no more,
However I begged at evening
When I counted my scanty store."

LUCKY BY CHOICE

"For Life is a just employer,
He gives you what you ask,
But once you have set the wages,
Why, you must bear the task."

"I worked for a menial's hire,
Only to learn, dismayed,
That any wage I had asked of Life,
Life would have willingly paid."

In my opinion, the moral of the poem is simply to demand more of yourself. Life is you!! You're going to get out of life what you bargain for. You don't get what you deserve, you get what you negotiate.

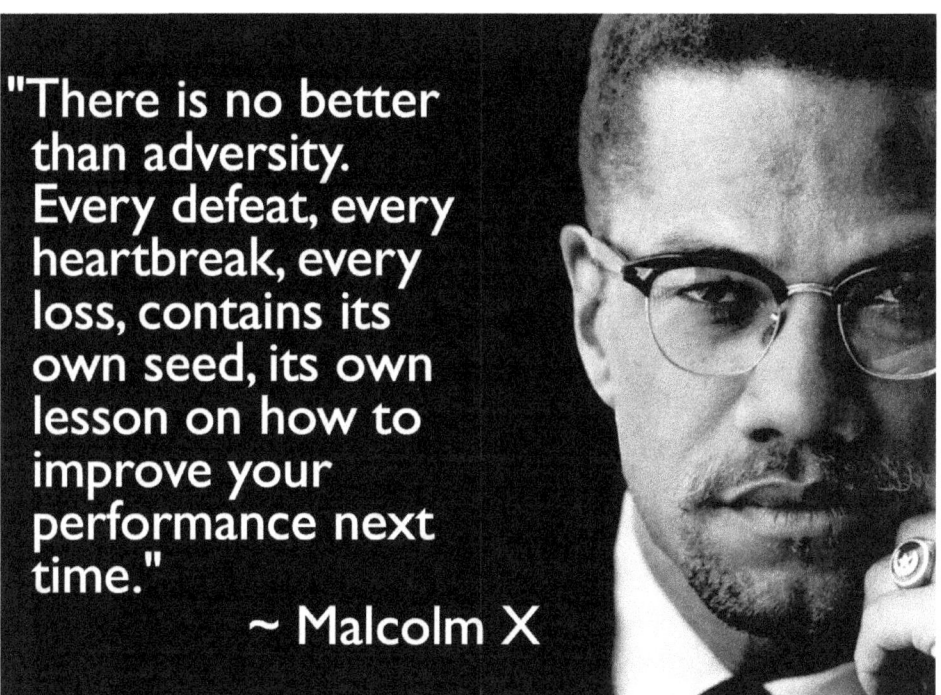

50. Knew Better, Do Better

"The test you are going through right now contains the opportunity for you to learn the appropriate lesson that you need at this point of your journey. If you truly learn the lesson in that struggle then you won't have to experience that lesson again. Fail to learn the lesson and life will provide another opportunity to learn it. This is why some disappointments seem to repeat in our lives. If you learned what you needed to the first time, you wouldn't need to be taught again."

This is an excerpt from Chapter 19, but I wanted to start with this to revisit it. In this chapter I want to talk about your knowledge, and your accountability of it. Simply put, you must apply the knowledge you possess. Having the knowledge is not enough. The application and proper use is what matters.

Life has its way of making sure that we get every lesson we need to so that we can do better than before. Experience is a good teacher. Let me correct that. Experience is an awesome, wonderful, great teacher!!!

A lot of times, we find ourselves lost in thought, questioning ourselves as to why we acted certain ways, as to why we made certain choices, why we said certain things, or why we didn't say certain things, why we changed or why we didn't. We ponder about what would have happened if only, if only we would have been different, done different, said different.

But Maya Angelou couldn't have said it better: "Do the best you can until you know better. Then when you know better, do better."

Do the best you can with what you know now. You'll learn more later. You'll learn more from doing. When you learn, then you can do better.

Continue to seek knowledge so that you may apply it in life.

Over the years, I have made some disastrous, bone-head mistakes; and taken some tremendous losses!! They didn't remain as such because I got the message out of the mistake, and the lesson from the loss. I was able to learn from those actions. I know better. As a result, I am now doing better.

I have a philosophy that I now stand on. It is, "Your education is your protection, and your advantage." Through gaining knowledge and education, you will learn what to do, when to do, how to do, where to do, why to do, and who to do it with. Those components and pockets of wisdom become your protection from making costly mistakes; as well as your advantage to get ahead in life.

>   The moment you know better,
>   you are expected to do better.

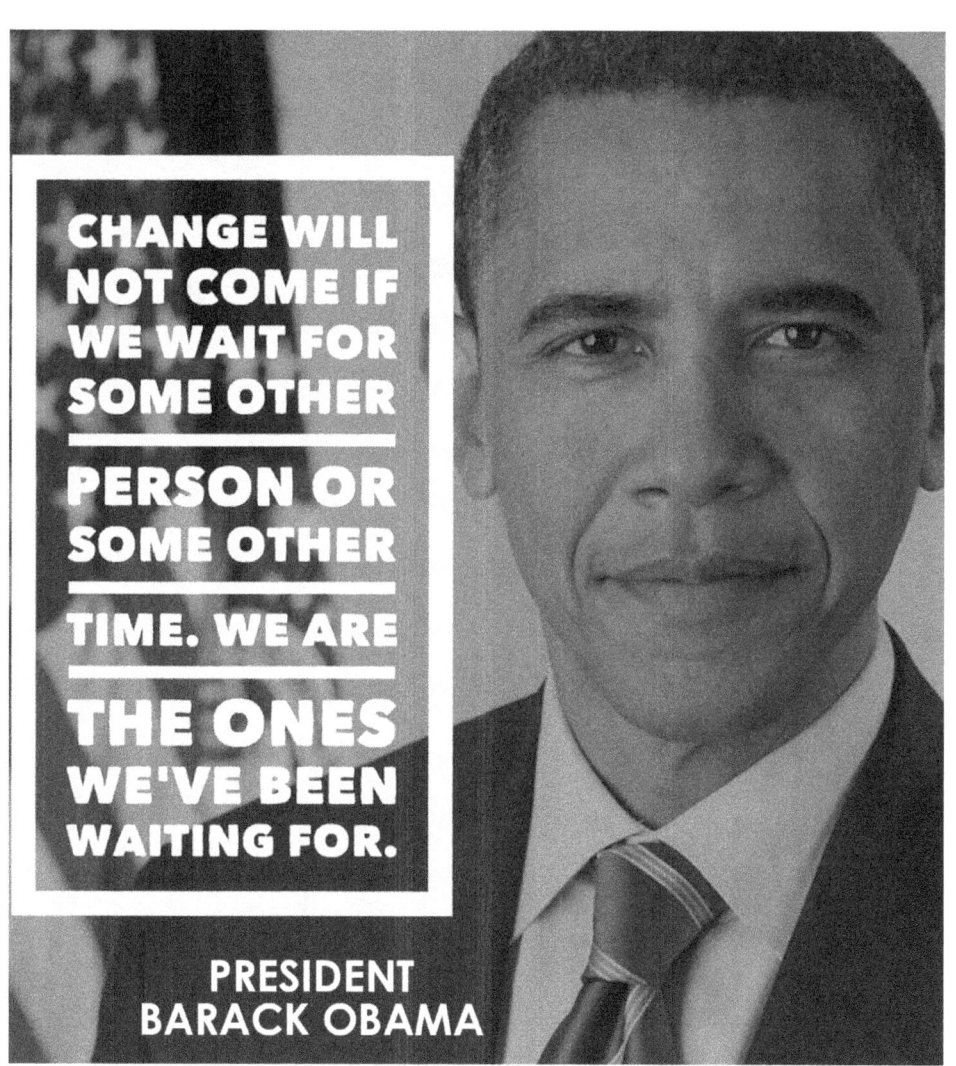

51. Nobody Owes You Anything

Life ain't lollipops, rainbows, and unicorns. Nobody said it would be easy, but it's damn sure worth it!!

When I was in the 4th grade at Charles Rice Elementary School in Dallas, Texas; I found a written piece by a guy named Keith Kennedy. I was 9 years old, what did I know about anything? I thought I knew a lot. As a matter of fact, now that I think about it, I did. I was ahead of my time. My life hadn't quite begun to form just yet, but I knew that I wanted great things out of life. Sure, I was what statistics called under-privileged, disenfranchised…hell, truth be told; poor. I knew it. It didn't matter to me though, because I wasn't missing what I never had.

Before I give you the message I want to give you, I want to share Keith Kennedy's piece with you. The Bottom Line……

FACE IT…Nobody owes you a living.
What you achieve or fail to achieve in your lifetime
is directly related to what you do or fail to do.
No one chooses his parents or childhood,
But you can choose your own direction!
Everyone has problems and obstacles to overcome,
But that too is relative to each individual.
NOTHING IS CARVED IN STONE…you can change
anything in your life if you want to bad enough.
Excuses are for losers. Those who take responsibility for
their actions are the real winners in life.
Winners meet life's challenges head on, knowing there are
no guarantees and give it all they've got.
And never think it's too late or too early to begin.

LUCKY BY CHOICE

Time plays no favorites and will pass whether you act or not.
TAKE CONTROL OF YOUR LIFE.
Dare to dream and take risks...Compete.
If you aren't willing to work for your goals, don't expect others to.
Believe In Yourself!!

And just like that, at 9 years old I became even more of a competitor in life. As you read this, and if you're older than 9 years of age (which you should be, if not, I'm impressed), I expect you to be taking life by the horns and dominating your journey to excellence, greatness, and success. Why? If I could do it at 9 years old, you can do it now!!

Success is for everybody, and nobody owes you anything. Whether you reach your goal or not, it's nobody's fault but your own. You are responsible for you. You have to put one foot in front of the other just like the next person has to. There is no free lunch being given.

Often times, people like to feel sorry for themselves. Maybe even have a pity party or two. Guess what, nobody cares!!! Stop playing victim to the circumstances you created. There's nobody to blame, but the person in the mirror.

Let's talk self-accountability for a moment, because this is what the chapter is about. When you have a well-developed sense of self-accountability, you are honest with yourself, and are answerable and responsible for what you say and do. You have the ability to look beyond the immediate moment to consider the consequences and know if you are willing to pay them.

How much of your success would you say is up to you—your choices, your actions, your behaviors—versus outside conditions?

51. Nobody Owes You Anything

If your mind-set is that you're at least 85% responsible for your success—and that just 15% depends on the way the wind blows—you'll likely be successful. If you blame your problems and failures—big or small, personal or professional—on other people, circumstances beyond your control, or just plain bad luck, you may be doomed to fail.

The good news? Accountability is not just a mind-set—it's also a skill-set that everyone can learn. It may not be as easy as one-two-three, but it is a three-step process:

1. Responsibility: It's not something you do—it's a way of thinking and being. When you're truly responsible, you believe that success or failure is up to you, even if you work within a team or are blind-sided by unforeseen circumstances. You own your commitment to a result before the fact, before you even take action.

2. Self-Empowerment: There is only one kind of empowerment, and that is self-empowerment. Unlike granting authority, empowerment comes from within. By empowering yourself, you take the actions—and the risks—to achieve a result and get what you want. Rather than waiting for someone to declare you empowered or give you that one lucky break, you step outside your comfort zone, make things happen, and answer for the outcomes.

3. Personal Accountability: Unlike responsibility (the "before") and self-empowerment (the "during"), personal accountability is the "after". It's a willingness to answer for the outcomes of your choices, actions, and behaviors. When you're personally accountable, you stop assigning blame, "should-ing" on people, and making excuses. Instead, you take the fall when your choices cause problems.

LUCKY BY CHOICE

At the end of the day, you will sink or swim because of your own ability. Don't expect anyone to come and save you. They don't have to, and they don't owe you. You will succeed, or not, on your own merit. You've read this a few times already, and now I give it to you again.......

>You are the master of your fate,
>and the captain of your soul.

Nobody owes you anything.........

52. The Choice Is Yours

We are now on the last mile of *this* journey of self-revelation, mental expansion, and personal development. As I stated before, this book is dedicated to you, and I want to sincerely thank you for the time you have shared with and given me. I hope that you have enjoyed each chapter, each nugget, each message, and each word. It is my wish that you have embraced the concepts of self-assessment, moral compassing, mindset shifting, and learning how to prepare to receive. My desire to provide you with those hidden gems as nuggets of wisdom was my attempt at sparking a flame of inspiration and prudence in your heart and soul.

As I close this labor of love, I want to challenge you, remind you, and encourage you to Tune In To Your Star Player; Try & Let Go; Check Your Expectations; Keep Yourself In Fighting Trim; Change Your Words, Change Your World; Wax On, Wax Off; Lose Yourself; Play To Win; and Take Charge!

If you are searching for a brand new life; I got news. It's going to cost you the old one. So let go of the past, and the past will let go of you. We are all an "ex" something; an ex-mistake maker, an ex-procrastinator, an ex-failure, maybe even an ex-con. You don't have to be the sharpest knife in the drawer. You just have to have dedication, discipline, excellence, integrity, and respect. You can be from Penn State or the State Pen, SUCCESS IS FOR EVERYBODY!!!

It is time to move forward in life towards your goals. No longer should you put your dreams on a shelf. Your life can be what you want it to be. If you will do for the next year what others will not; you will do for the rest of your life what others cannot.

People too often forget that it is your own choice how you want to spend the rest of your life. Success is never an accident. You have to want it. You have to plan it. You have to do what successful people do. Not just read. Not just look or like. You have to DO!!!

Martin Luther King, Jr. said, "The ultimate measure of a man is not where he stands in moments of comfort and convenience, but where he stands in times of challenge and controversy."

Ease is a greater threat to progress than hardship. There will be challenges, mountains to climb, obstacles to overcome, and burdens to bear. Winning is in your blood, you were born with what it takes to succeed. Don't just compete, dominate!

Remember what Muhammad Ali said, "Impossible is just a big word thrown around by small men who find it easier to live in the world they've been given than to explore the power they have to change it. Impossible is not a fact. It's an opinion. Impossible is not a declaration. It's a dare. Impossible is potential. Impossible is temporary. Impossible is nothing!!

In Tony Robbins' best-seller, Unlimited Power….. he says "The birth of excellence begins with our awareness that our beliefs are a choice. We usually don't think of it that way, but belief can be a conscious choice. You can choose beliefs that limit you, or you can choose beliefs that support you. The trick is to choose the beliefs that are conducive to success and the results you want; and then discard the ones that hold you back."

52. The Choice Is Yours

Life is all about decisions; your decisions. You are your savior. Change will not come if you wait for some other person or some other time. You are the one you've been waiting for. You are the change that you seek. Yes, it will cost a lot of things; but who cares about the price of the shovel when you are standing on a gold mine…dig in!!!!

Today is the first day of the rest of your life. Make the rest of your life the best of your life. The Choice Is Yours……

About The Author

Assertive, confident, creative, determined, innovative, and trendsetter are just a few of the definitive measures and characteristics that make up this Award Winning, Lifetime Entrepreneur; Author; Certified Life Coach; Motivational Speaker; Real Estate Investor; and Philanthropist. Keio Gamble was born and raised in Dallas, Texas with humble beginnings. Keio set lofty goals at an early age. He vowed that he would become the epitome of success. Staying focused on education and personal development, Keio graduated from Wilmer-Hutchins High School in 1994, received his Bachelor of Science Degree from Prairie View A&M University in 1998, served eight years in the US Army Reserves from 1996 to 2004, and is a proud member of the prestigious Omega Psi Phi Fraternity, Incorporated – initiated at the Rho Theta Chapter in the Spring of 1996.

Due to an arsenal of cutting-edge qualities, forward thinking, and integrated techniques that make him a force to be reckoned with, he has been highly sought out to provide his expertise and solutions as a consultant, motivational speaker, and certified life coach in the matters of leadership, self-improvement, entrepreneurship, and team-building.

With proven success at integrating life experiences, recognizing opportunity, motivating the masses, and continuing to pioneer and spearhead movements that impact the growth and development of the people and communities he comes in contact with; Keio has cemented his position as an influential veteran in his industries, while his expertise has him considered as a mover and shaker.

Known as an alchemist, Keio is devoted to being a humble, servant leader and bridge-builder. His goal in life is to leave a legacy that will benefit his family, friends, associates, and all that will come after him.

As an exemplary visionary, Keio hopes that through his unparalleled work ethic, professionalism, ambition and fortitude; he will be an inspiration to others and prove that dedication, discipline, excellence, integrity, and respect are the keys to success.

:For More Information About The Author:
www.KeioGamble.com

www.ingramcontent.com/pod-product-compliance
Lightning Source LLC
Chambersburg PA
CBHW070538010526
44118CB00012B/1163